DATE DUE			
JAN 0 4 1999			

```
J                        9/94
970.1   Force, Roland W.
Force   The American
        Indians
```

THE AMERICAN INDIANS

Consulting Editors

Ann Orlov
Managing Editor, Harvard
Encyclopedia of American
Ethnic Groups

M. Mark Stolarik
*President, The Balch Institute
for Ethnic Studies, Philadelphia*

Daniel Patrick Moynihan
*U.S. Senator from New York,
Senior Consulting Editor*

THE AMERICAN INDIANS

Roland W. Force
and
Maryanne Tefft Force

CHELSEA HOUSE PUBLISHERS

New York Philadelphia

On the cover: A group of Indians poses for a photographer in the late 19th century.

CHELSEA HOUSE PUBLISHERS

Editor-in-Chief: Remmel Nunn
Managing Editor: Karyn Gullen Browne
Copy Chief: Juliann Barbato
Picture Editor: Adrian G. Allen
Art Director: Maria Epes
Deputy Copy Chief: Mark Rifkin
Assistant Art Director: Noreen Romano
Manufacturing Manager: Gerald Levine
Systems Manager: Lindsey Ottman
Production Manager: Joseph Romano
Production Coordinator: Marie Claire Cebrián

The Peoples of North America

Senior Editor: Kathy Kuhtz

Staff for THE AMERICAN INDIANS

Associate Editor: Scott Prentzas
Copy Editor: John Wisniewski
Picture Researcher: Wendy P. Wills
Cover Illustration: Paul Biniasz
Banner Design: Hrana Janto

3   5   7   9   8   6   4

Library of Congress Cataloging-in-Publication Data

Force, Roland W.
   The American Indians/Roland W. Force and Maryanne Tefft Force.
      p. cm.—(The peoples of North America)
   Includes bibliographical references and index.
   Summary: Discusses the history, culture and religion of the North American Indians,
their place in American society, and the problems they face as an ethnic group in North
America.
   ISBN 0-87754-860-9
      0-7910-0280-2 (pbk.)
   1. Indians of North America—Juvenile literature. [1. Indians of North America.]
I. Force, Maryanne. II. Title. III. Series.   90-2259
E77.F69 1990   CIP
305.897′073—dc20   AC

CONTENTS

THE PEOPLES OF NORTH AMERICA

CHELSEA HOUSE PUBLISHERS

A NATION
OF NATIONS

Daniel Patrick Moynihan

The Constitution of the United States begins: "We the People of the United States. . ." Yet, as we know, the United States was not then and is not now made up of a single group of people. It is made up of many peoples. Immigrants and bondsmen from Europe, Asia, Africa, and Central and South America came here or were brought here, and still they come. They forged one nation and made it their own. More than 100 years ago, Walt Whitman expressed this great central fact of America: "Here is not merely a nation, but a teeming Nation of nations."

Although the ingenuity and acts of courage of these immigrants, our ancestors, shaped the North American way of life, we sometimes take their contributions for granted. This fine series, *The Peoples of North America*, examines the experiences and contributions of different immigrant groups and how these contributions determined the future of the United States and Canada.

Immigrants did not abandon their ethnic traditions when they reached the shores of North America. Each ethnic group had its own customs and traditions, and each brought different experiences, accomplishments, skills, values, styles of dress, and tastes in food that lingered long after its arrival. Yet this profusion of differences created a singularity, or bond, among the immigrants.

The United States and Canada are unusual in this respect. Whereas religious and ethnic differences have sparked intolerance throughout the rest of the world—from the 17th-century religious wars to the 19th-century nationalist movements in Europe to the near extermination of the Jewish people under Nazi Germany—North Americans have struggled to learn how to respect each other's differences and live in harmony.

Our two countries are hardly the only two in which different groups must learn to live together. There is no nation of significant size anywhere in the world which would not be classified as multi-ethnic. But only in North America are there so *many* different groups, most of them living cheek by jowl with one another.

This is not easy. Look around the world. And it has not always been easy for us. Witness the exclusion of Chinese immigrants, and for practical purposes Japanese also, in the late 19th century. But by the late 20th century, Chinese and Japanese Americans were the most successful of all the groups recorded by the census. We have had prejudice aplenty, but it has been resisted and recurrently overcome.

The remarkable ability of Americans to live together as one people was seriously threatened by the issue of slavery. Thousands of settlers from the British Isles had arrived in the colonies as indentured servants, agreeing to work for a specified number of years on farms or as apprentices in return for passage to America and room and board. When the first Africans arrived in the then-British colonies during the 17th century, some colonists thought that they too should be treated as indentured servants. Eventually, the question of whether the Africans should be treated as indentured, like the English, or as slaves who could be owned for life was considered in a Maryland court. The court's calamitous decree held that blacks were slaves bound to a lifelong servitude, and so also were their children. America went through a time of moral examination and civil war before it finally freed African slaves and their descendants. The principle that all people are created equal had faced its greatest challenge and survived.

Yet the court ruling that set blacks apart from other races fanned flames of discrimination that burned long after slavery was abolished—and that still flicker today. Indeed, it was about the time of the American Civil War that European theories of evolution were turned to the service of ranking different peoples by their presumed distance from our apelike ancestors.

When the Irish flooded American cities to escape the famine in Ireland, the cartoonists caricatured the typical "Paddy" (a common term for Irish immigrants) as an apelike creature with jutting jaw and sloping forehead.

By the 20th century, racism and ethnic prejudice had given rise to virulent theories of a Northern European master race. When Adolf Hitler came to power in Germany in 1933, he popularized the notion of an Aryan race. Only a man of the deepest ignorance and evil could have done this. *Aryan* is a Sanskrit word, which is to say the ancient script of what we now think of as India. It means "noble" and was adopted by linguists—notably by a fine German scholar, Max Müller—to denote the Indo-European family of languages. Müller was horrified that anyone could think of it in terms of race, especially a race of blond-haired, blue-eyed Teutons. But the Nazis embraced the notion of a master race. Anyone with darker and heavier features was considered inferior. Buttressed by these theories, the German Nazi state from 1933 to 1945 set out to destroy European Jews, along with Poles, Gypsies, Russians, and other groups considered inferior. It nearly succeeded. Millions of these people were murdered.

The tragedies brought on by ethnic and racial intolerance throughout the world demonstrate the importance of North America's efforts to create a society free of prejudice and inequality.

A relatively recent example of the New World's desire to resolve ethnic friction nonviolently is the solution that the Canadians found to a conflict between two ethnic groups. A long-standing dispute as to whether Canadian culture was properly English or French resurfaced in the mid-1960s, dividing the peoples of the French-speaking Province of Quebec from those of the English-speaking provinces. Relations grew tense, then bitter, then violent. The Royal Commission on Bilingualism and Biculturalism was established to study the growing crisis and to propose measures to ease the tensions. As a result of the commission's recommendations, all official documents and statements from the national government's capital at Ottawa are now issued in both French and English, and bilingual education is encouraged.

The year 1980 marked a coming of age for the United States's ethnic heritage. For the first time, the U.S. Bureau of the Census asked people about their ethnic background. Americans chose from more than 100 groups, including French Basque, Spanish Basque, French Canadian, African-American, Peruvian, Armenian, Chinese, and Japanese. The ethnic group with the largest response was English (49.6 million). More than 100 million Americans claimed ancestors from the British Isles, which includes England, Ireland, Wales, and Scotland. There were almost as many Germans (49.2 million) as English. The Irish-American population (40.2 million) was third, but the next-largest ethnic group, the African-Americans, was a distant fourth (21 million). There was a sizable group of French ancestry (13 million) as well as of Italian (12 million). Poles, Dutch, Swedes, Norwegians, and Russians followed. These groups, and other smaller ones, represent the wondrous profusion of ethnic influences in North America.

Canada too has learned more about the diversity of its population. Studies conducted during the French/English conflict showed that Canadians were descended from Ukrainians, Germans, Italians, Chinese, Japanese, native Indians, and Inuit, among others. Canada found it had no ethnic majority, although nearly half of its immigrant population had come from the British Isles. Canada, like the United States, is a land of immigrants for whom mutual tolerance is a matter of reason as well as principle. But note how difficult this can be in practice, even for persons of manifest goodwill.

The people of North America are the descendants of one of the greatest migrations in history. And that migration is not over.

Archaeologists uncover mammoth remains at an excavation site near Dent, Colorado, in 1933. Chipped-stone projectile points were found along with the mammoth bones, providing strong evidence that humans lived in North America at least 10,000 years ago. Although there is much dispute over the timing of the first migration to North America, most scientists estimate that humans first reached the Americas between 50,000 and 10,000 years ago.

THE FIRST AMERICANS

Humans ranged across the Old World for thousands of years, leaving behind sufficient skeletal remains to reveal their general, although incomplete, evolution from ancient forms. However, because only the remains of modern humans have been found in the Americas, a majority of archaeologists (scientists who study the remains of past human societies) have concluded that modern humans must have evolved elsewhere and then migrated to the New World at a relatively later date.

Most scientists now believe that North and South America were populated by people who migrated from Asia long ago, although there is considerable disagreement as to when they first arrived. For many years, archaeologists assumed that humans had been in the New World for only a few thousand years. Although there is no consensus among scholars, the majority now estimate that humans first reached the Americas sometime between 50,000 to 10,000 years ago. The bitter

This chipped-stone projectile point was among those found with bison bones in Folsom, New Mexico, in 1927. Folsom points tipped the spears of Paleoindians approximately 10,000 years ago, and their discovery forced scientists to reconsider their theories about how and when humans arrived in North America.

dispute between archaeologists over when people first migrated to the Americas arose more that 50 years ago when some astonishing findings definitively placed humans in the New World thousands of years earlier than had been previously assumed.

A New Theory of Migration Emerges

Until the late 1920s, most scientists believed that people had arrived in the New World from other continents by sailing across the oceans. Some scientists, however, thought that people might have made the highly dangerous journey across the pack ice of the far North on foot. Two accidental discoveries of stone projectile points in New Mexico support the latter theory.

In the spring of 1908, a cowboy noticed some bones jutting out of a bank of an arroyo, or gully, while he was looking for lost cattle near Folsom, New Mexico. He retrieved some projectile points that looked different from the usual arrowheads of the area and some bones that seemed larger than those of cattle. His inquisitiveness ultimately led to proof that humans had been in the New World for thousands of years longer than had been supposed. Subsequent excavations at the Folsom site, beginning in 1926, unearthed a number of important artifacts that forced scientists to revise their notions concerning migration theory and the date that habitation of the Americas actually began. Among the artifacts discovered was a projectile point found between the ribs of a type of bison believed to have become extinct about 10,000 years ago. Scientists concluded that because a handmade object had actually killed the animal (or contributed to its death), humans must have been present in the New World prior to the animal's extinction.

A few years later, in 1932, another startling discovery was made near Clovis, New Mexico. Reminiscent of the Folsom site, handmade weapons were found with animal bones thousands of years old—this time, bones of mammoths, camels, and a type of horse. Several of these now extinct animals had projectile points lodged between their ribs, providing further direct evidence that humans populated North America at least 12,000 years ago, centuries earlier than had previously been thought.

Although the Clovis and Folsom projectile points differ in some respects—for example, the Clovis points are longer and heavier—they share important characteristics. The most distinctive of these is that each has a groove (*flute*) running the length of both sides, prompting scientists to term them both fluted points. More Folsom points were later found in a number of locations, primarily in the southern Great Plains. In contrast, Clovis points have been uncovered throughout North America from Alaska to Mexico and from coast to coast, but none have yet been discovered in Asia.

Archaeologists do not know the names of the peoples who made these points but have generally used the term *Fluted-point People* to refer to both the Clovis People (those using Clovis points) and the Folsom

Clovis points (named after a New Mexico site where stone projectiles of this type were first discovered) such as this one unearthed in Nebraska are slender, flat, sharp-edged, and fluted. (Lengthwise channels have been chipped into each side of the point.)

People (those using Folsom points). The Fluted-point People were a part of a much larger group of Native Americans whom scientists call Paleoindians.

Major Migrations to North America

On the basis of physiological, archaeological, and linguistic data, many scientists believe that there were possibly three major migrations to the New World. The first, they hypothesize, was by Paleoindians, who passed through Beringia (the landmass composed of the Bering land bridge and part of Alaska) at least 14,000 to 12,000 years ago when the sea level was lowered by glaciation. Paleoindians then moved across much of present-day Canada and the United States. Some continued their journey and ultimately established settlements throughout most of North and South America by 12,000 to 11,500 years ago. However, as researchers unearth new sites with much older dates, theories concerning the dates of arrival and subsequent settlement patterns remain controversial.

Some scientists have suggested that Paleoindians may have had an earlier *lithic* (stone) technology that preceded the one that produced fluted points. They believe that the various crudely worked stone implements that have been unearthed for many years were made and used by Paleoindians before they developed more sophisticated fluted points. If these objects are indeed handmade, then they provide further evidence that humans arrived in the New World at an earlier date. A number of scholars still dispute whether or not these objects were handmade. These scholars argue that although Paleoindians may have used these earlier objects, they did not manufacture them but rather selected them from nature because of their utility. They also believe that these objects coexisted with fluted points.

Archaeologists believe that a second wave of immigrants brought a different technology with them approximately 10,000 years ago. Scholars refer to certain of their tools as *microblades*, which have been found primarily in Alaskan and eastern Siberian sites. Some researchers maintain that these migrants were the ancestors of Northwest Coast and Athapaskan peoples. A third wave of people are thought by some to have followed at a similar early date. These may have been the forebears of the Inuit (the officially adopted name for all Eskimo) and Aleut people who settled along the coasts of Alaska and the chain of islands called the Aleutians. At Ushki, a site located in the Kamchatka River valley in the Soviet Union, scientists have discovered handmade materials that date to 14,000 years ago and demonstrate a lengthy occupation of the region. The oldest finds include tools and human burials with stone pendants and beads.

The Bering Land Bridge

The discoveries of the Clovis and Folsom points forced scientists to rethink their ideas about the time of migration to the New World and to develop a theoretical approach that would take into account the new findings. The idea of watercraft as being the major means of migration was discarded. Instead, the notion was advanced that if people were in the New World by 12,000 to 10,000 years ago, they must have come on foot over the ancient land bridge that connected North America with Asia. The word *bridge* is misleading because it suggests a narrow passage connecting two places. Actually, the Bering land bridge was 1,000 miles wide in some places.

Because of glaciation during the period popularly known as the Ice Age (which began about 2.5 million years ago and ended about 10,000 years ago), the level of the sea was sometimes at least 330 feet lower than it is today. During this period, enormous amounts of seawater were removed from the oceans through evaporation, which caused the formation of immense glaciers and ice sheets on land. In the process, the con-

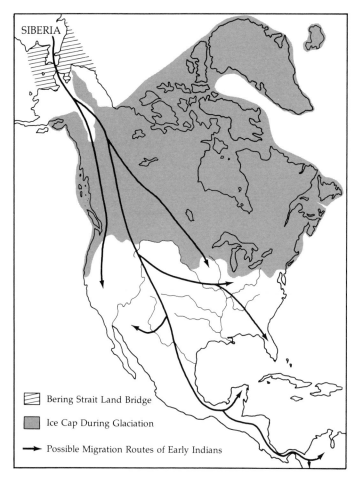

Bering Strait Land Bridge

Ice Cap During Glaciation

→ Possible Migration Routes of Early Indians

tours of the earth's land masses became altered. Over time, as the earth periodically became warmer, the water returned to the oceans as the ice packs melted. During these interglacial stages, the coastal shelves and other shallow ocean regions that had been exposed were inundated once more and the contours of the continents changed accordingly. Depending upon the extent of warming, the rising sea level also inundated the land bridge between Asia and North America. Today the United States and the Soviet Union are separated by a stretch of water called the Bering Strait, which is only about 55 miles wide at its narrowest point. It is a shallow passage averaging only about 90 to 160 feet in depth.

Many prehistorians continue to hypothesize that hunters first set foot on the land bridge in search of game animals that presumedly lived there. Ultimately, the descendants of those intrepid hunters moved across the region, arriving in present-day Alaska. Having crossed the bridge, the people and the animals they hunted were sealed off from the more temperate lands to the south by glacial ice that spanned the North American continent. Then, only after thousands of years, when warming trends caused the glacial ice to recede, humans and animals moved southward.

Whereas scholars debate over the evidence for antiquity, many Native Americans maintain their own understandings of their origins. They staunchly believe that their origins were in the New World. Native American creation legends recount in epic fashion the emergence of human life in North America as something bequeathed by supernatural powers—something that is unnecessary to prove or qualify.

Petroglyphs on a sandstone outcropping in Wyoming provide a glimpse into the life of ancient Indians. Knowledge about the first inhabitants of North America comes from the large array of objects that they made or used.

ANCIENT INDIANS

Because scant human remains attest to their presence, very little is known about the earliest people who occupied the Western Hemisphere. Scientists can only offer theories about their family life, religious beliefs, and social organizations. Knowledge about the first North Americans comes primarily from the objects that they made and used, such as ornaments, tools, and weapons. Evidence of early human occupation also consists of remnants of campfires and garbage dumps, house-post holes, and even fecal matter found in arid caves. Humans also left behind an impressive record of their existence in such things as pictographs and petroglyphs (drawings or engravings in stone), structures, trails and roads, and graves containing burial objects. Artifacts that have been unearthed attest to the great skill and ingenuity of ancient artisans, who not only created magnificent works of art but also made everyday objects that were beautiful as well as functional.

Archaeologists have termed the first great sequence of the presence of humans in the New World the Lithic period, which is also known as the Paleoindian period. The earliest date for this era is still shrouded in mystery, but it could be as early as 50,000 years ago. The period ended about 5000 B.C. The Archaic (or Foraging) period was much shorter by comparison, lasting from about 5000 to 1000 B.C. The subsequent Formative period was even more brief, lasting from 1000 B.C. to A.D. 1000.

The Paleoindian, Archaic, and Formative periods differed in important ways. Although each period shared some basic similarities with the others, people constantly made changes in how they lived, and not all made the same choices. And some groups, because of the nature of the region in which they lived, were more restricted in their choices. For these reasons, the nature and sequences of cultural change differed from place to place.

The Paleoindians shared certain common origins, but over time they became very diverse culturally, linguistically, and to some extent physically. The enormous diversification that typifies Native Americans required both the passage of time and the relative isolation of groups so that unique features of culture, language, and physical characteristics could develop in different ways. By the end of the Formative period, different groups had developed distinctive cultural adaptations to the various environments across North America, and they had begun to organize into small family bands, tribes, confederacies, and nations.

The Paleoindian Period

For much of the Paleoindian period, the climate of the earth greatly differed from what it is today. By 10,000 years ago, the great masses of glacial ice had melted, leaving in their wake rivers and lakes of all sizes. In

North America, some areas that are deserts today were swamps or grasslands. The abundant flora provided food for countless animals, and the flourishing herds in turn supplied sustenance for humans. Scientists do not know precisely how much the human population grew, but the food supply enabled it to multiply rapidly. By A.D. 1000, settlements existed all across North America.

The Paleoindian period is characterized by a way of life that depended on the hunting of big game. In addition to small game, there were huge herds of grazing animals—deer, elk, and such now extinct species as giant beavers and bison, camels, and woolly mammoths. The first Americans needed to follow the herds for survival, and to the extent their game migrated seasonally they, too, migrated. However, there were regional differences in the degree to which people were nomadic. Large grazing herds roamed across the vast plains of North America, and the hunters followed. In contrast, the heavily forested eastern part of the continent provided a stable population of small game animals that enabled hunters and their families to establish relatively permanent homes.

The Clovis People were one of the successful hunting groups. Their fluted flint points were excellent for piercing the hides of the great mammals. Another implement of great importance also associated with the Clovis People is the *atlatl,* or spear-thrower. The device consisted of a short shaft with a pin or hook at the end that bore upon the butt of the spear shaft. The atlatl served to lengthen the thrower's arm and thereby increased the velocity and force of the spear's forward thrust.

A large mammal, such as a mammoth, served as more than just food. Its hide could be made into garments or shelters, its bones could be formed into tools, weapons, and ornaments, and the meat could provide for a sizable band of people. The beast's size even determined the nature of the hunt. A team effort was required to bring down a mammoth. Each hunter had to know his or her role. Men and women might have used a small

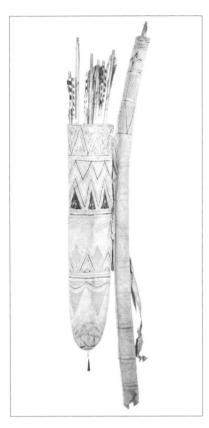

The advent of the bow and arrow approximately 5,500 years ago greatly enhanced the hunting efficiency of ancient Indians.

needle made from one of the animal's bones as they fashioned a robe from its hide while a large chunk of its flesh roasted over a fire. So often, tools such as small bone needles and awls have been lost over the centuries. Stone weapons of warfare or the hunt have generally been the ones that have survived. By 6000 or 5000 B.C., the great beasts had all become extinct. Whether they were hunted out or whether the climate was a factor in their demise is uncertain. At least 5,500 years ago, a new technology—the bow and arrow—emerged and immediately revolutionized hunting. A bow could propel an arrow with tremendous power and bring down animals at great distances. And a parcel of arrows and a bow could easily be carried and be put into service quickly. Most scientists believe this technology was developed in the Old World and transported to the New World. However, it may have been an independent invention by Native Americans.

As the climate became warmer during the Paleoindian period, a greater wealth of marine life emerged in the ocean waters. Using some type of watercraft, people could now hunt and fish at sea as well as on the lakes and rivers. Boats made of hide and birch-bark canoes made humans mobile and even more formidable in their pursuit of prey. As the Paleoindian period ended, humans had begun to expand their sources of food out of necessity, more actively gathering fruits and berries, edible grasses, and seeds. A remarkable array of edible plant products—wild berries, seeds, fruits, and nuts— were also abundant in the temperate climates of areas located south of Alaska and Canada. Although agriculture was not yet practiced, people undoubtedly noticed the seasonal presence of various plants and moved about to harvest them.

The Archaic Period

In the 1920s, archaeologists discovered evidence of a group of people who lived about 9,000 years ago near

Cochise in southeastern Arizona. By the end of the Paleoindian period, the Cochise, as they came to be called, gathered or foraged for various seeds and nuts, which they then ground on millstones to produce a flourlike substance. Along with weaving skills, the Cochise developed some elementary pottery techniques and made crude pottery figurines. They may have been the forerunners of the Southwest cultures of a later period.

Not only were the Cochise experienced food-gatherers, but they may have been among the first farmers in North America. In Bat Cave, located in New Mexico, scientists have recovered Cochise-style weapons alongside tiny, inch-long corncobs. The cobs were not from wild corn but came from a primitive domesticated species. The Cochise either domesticated this hybrid type themselves or borrowed kernels from another tribe for their own gardens. Corn, as it is known today, was originally a wild grass, but over time it was developed into a grain. One theory is that corn was cultivated in some part of present-day Mexico, perhaps in the Tehuacán Valley, and that corn growing spread north into the southwestern United States. At some point, Indians began to select certain strains for replanting. Ultimately, corn produced such thick husks that it could no longer reproduce itself unless humans planted the corn kernels.

During the Archaic period, another culture stretched eastward from present-day Missouri to Kentucky, southward to Alabama and Florida, and northward to New England and southern Canada. The people who lived in this area, known as the Eastern Woodland, adapted to a series of different environments and relied upon a wide range of plants and animals. Stone tools and ornaments were both chipped and ground by using stones or other tools. Some of the most attractive objects made by stoneworkers are the so-called birdstones, believed to be decorative balancing weights that were affixed to spear-throwers.

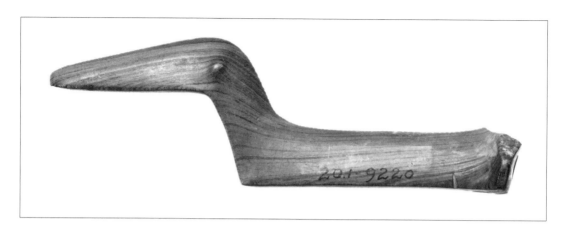

Ancient Indian stoneworkers made decorative balancing weights known as birdstones, such as this one discovered in Indiana. Hunters strapped birdstones to the flexible shafts of their spear-throwers to provide greater leverage for their throws.

To the west, in the upper Great Lakes area in what is now the state of Wisconsin, another group of Archaic people became metalworkers. They traded their copper products to other groups as far away as present-day Florida and New York. Archaeologists believe that the animals these people hunted migrated north to avoid increasingly hotter weather and, as a result, the Old Copper culture, as it has been called, disappeared about 3,000 years ago. Copper artifacts were not seen again until the Hopewell culture period.

The Formative Period

The Archaic period did not come to an abrupt end. Rather, those people who had already begun to develop settled communities continued the process in the Formative period, which began about 1000 B.C. In many places, the people continued to reside in the same general location, which therefore provided archaeologists with a more comprehensive view of their existence.

The Formative period is marked by the dramatic impact of agriculture on human populations. Agriculture enabled relatively large numbers of people to settle in permanent communities. Shelters became more substantial, and villages, towns, and even cities emerged. The development of permanent communities led to a number of alterations in social organization. By 1000 B.C., the varied peoples of North America had grown greatly in numbers. Trade flourished as products or goods from one region were exchanged for those from another. People were influenced by the ways of others, frequently borrowing ideas, technologies, and goods and altering their own culture in the process. In the years that followed, pottery making, agricultural practices, and the use of smoking pipes and tobacco as important ceremonial implements gradually developed and spread.

Perhaps the most spectacular development in the Formative period was the construction of burial mounds. There was not a single mound-building culture. Instead, there were many peoples who created earthen mounds over a long span of time. The oldest mounds in North America are found along the Atlantic coast from Florida to South Carolina. Ring-shaped mounds constructed of shells are located on an island off the Georgia coast and contain the first evidence of pottery in North America. It is so remarkably akin to pots found in similar shell mounds along the coast of Colombia that some scientists have concluded Indians must have made long coastal voyages as early as 2400 B.C., bringing cultural influences northward.

Serpent Mound winds along a hilltop in Ohio. The mound was built about 2,000 years ago by the Adena people, who were the earliest mound builders. Early Indians built thousands of burial mounds throughout the United States.

Religious rites, especially those associated with death, became more elaborate during the Archaic period. Among the earliest burial mounds discovered were those excavated at Indian Knoll, an Archaic period site in Kentucky dating to 3000 B.C. Tombs continued as the principal purpose for mounds until A.D. 500–700, when flat-topped mounds were constructed primarily as bases for temples. Some mounds consisted of giant animal-effigy earthworks. In Ohio, for example, a sinuous mound a quarter of a mile long depicts a snake.

The Adena People, the snake-mound builders, lived mostly in the Ohio Valley from about 1000 B.C. to about A.D. 200. They built mounds by constructing shallow earthworks atop burials. Subsequently, the practice was emphasized more, and the funeral mounds became enormous. The building of these large mounds required the labor of many people. This, in turn, required a complex social organization and a power structure.

Skeletal remains tell something of the Adena People. They were exceedingly tall—women averaged six feet in height, men seven—and had round heads in contrast to most other groups who were long-headed. These characteristics and some of their ceremonial behavior suggest that the Adena People emigrated from some distant place such as Mexico. There is no clear evidence that they practiced agriculture, but they made stone tobacco pipes, pottery, and jewelry.

Around 500 to 100 B.C., the Hopewell People developed and eventually supplanted or displaced the Adena, ultimately occupying an area extending from the Gulf of Mexico to the Great Lakes. For 1,000 years, the Hopewell People dominated the Midwest, creating objects of great beauty—carvings in wood and bone; woven mats; and ornaments of mica, copper, gold, and silver. They clothed themselves elegantly in woven cloth, furs, and hides and had a class system and craft guilds. They were proficient traders, taking full advantage of their central location and creating trading centers to which people came from distant places to barter. Hopewell artisans used materials from afar, including huge conch shells from the Gulf of Mexico, copper from the Great Lakes, and obsidian from Wyoming. The Hopewell People also built huge burial mounds in present-day New York, Ohio, and Illinois.

Hopewell culture diminished around A.D. 600, and another agricultural people began its own reign of greatness. Mississippian culture, as it has been termed, began its ascendance in the rich river lands of the lower Mississippi Valley and spread to riverine sites in Oklahoma, Illinois, Wisconsin, Alabama, Ohio, Tennessee, and North Carolina. Some of the features of this culture are reminiscent of Mexico: pyramidal, flat-topped temple mounds built around a central plaza; ritual activity centering on death; the existence of ruler-priests; and the use of feathered serpent figures in art.

The largest Mississippian culture mound—100 feet high, 1,000 feet long, and more than 700 feet wide—is located at Cahokia, Illinois. The Cahokia settlement appears to have reached its zenith around 1200, but by the time of European arrival it had ceased to exist. At its peak, as many as 40,000 people are thought to have lived in or near Cahokia. It was a religious and trade center unsurpassed by any other Mississippian community. Wealthy aristocrats and priests ruled over commoners, who tilled the fields, built the mounds, and served their masters. Servants were sacrificed and buried with their rulers. The rise of Mississippian culture is a prime example of how a society can develop when it has a large food base. In contrast, people in such regions as the Great Basin (present-day Nevada and Utah) with its unproductive environment, remained at a bare subsistence level during the same period. Mere survival was a full-time occupation.

At about the same time Mississippian culture developed, the Hohokam, Mogollon, and Anasazi cultures were taking form in southern Utah, Colorado, Arizona, New Mexico, and northern Mexico. These cultures differed from the Mississippian as well as from each other, but they shared an important likeness. Each had developed a productive agricultural system and had a food base on which to build their own distinctive cultures.

The ancestors of the Hohokam may have been the ancient Cochise People who were early settlers in the region, but some scientists believe that the Hohokam were the descendants of Mexican immigrants, primarily because they had so many things that originated in Mexico. Among them were corn, cotton, irrigation techniques, pottery styles, carved shells, turquoise mosaics, ball courts, platform mounds, and copper bells.

Along the Gila River, which cuts across southern Arizona on its way to the Gulf of California, the Hohokam built a massive irrigation system that brought water to the parched land. They designed and constructed deep, narrow canals, dams, flumes, and floodgates and lined their ditches with clay to confine the water. The Hohokam went beyond being agriculturists; they were master engineers who were able to control water with the simplest of tools. After flourishing for years, the Hohokam abandoned their settlements, most likely because of a severe drought. Their descendants, the Pima and the Papago, who occupy the same region today, call them the Vanished Ones.

To the east of the Hohokam, in New Mexico on the banks of the Rio Grande, the Mogollon People lived in mountain valleys at about the same time. They farmed, but not to the same extent as the Hohokam did, and supplemented their diet with hunting and gathering. The Mogollon grew corn, squash, beans, and tobacco. Like the Hohokam, their life-style was also similar to the ancient Cochise. The Mogollon are known for their pit houses, which were well adapted to the daily fluctuations of heat and cold in the region.

The Mogollon People's greatest legacy is their pottery. The Mogollon in the Mimbres area in southwestern New Mexico produced a remarkable ware distinguished by imaginative stylized animals, insects, and

human figures. Their dead were always buried with a bowl over the head. Each piece used in this way was "killed" by punching a hole in its bottom. The Mogollon People also innovated a new form of housing around A.D. 1100. They abandoned their pit houses and built rambling, single-story adobe buildings that the Spanish later called *pueblos*. Such a structure might contain 50 rooms and house many families. The Mogollon finally abandoned their settlements, moving northward to mix with the Anasazi People they found there. The Zuni of today are possibly descendants of the Mogollon.

The Anasazi, which means Old Ones in the Navajo language, were the cliff dwellers of the Four Corners region where the states of Utah, Colorado, Arizona, and New Mexico meet. Famous sites such as Mesa Verde in Colorado and the White House ruins of Canyon de Chelly in Arizona are places where the Anasazi built their abodes in the mouths of huge, dry caves and under the overhang of steep rock canyon walls. The arid climate and long years of isolation preserved many of their culture objects, which provide a rich archaeological record.

Like other people in the region, the Anasazi were initially prefarming and preceramic. At first, they were

The Mimbres Mogollon, who lived in present-day New Mexico, are well known for their distinctive black-on-white pottery decorated with geometric designs. The Mimbres Mogollon always buried their dead with a bowl over the corpse's head, and each bowl was then "killed" by punching a hole in its bottom.

hunters and gatherers but began cultivating corn and establishing more settled communities about 1000 B.C. Like the Mogollon, the Anasazi also lived in pit houses, but about A.D. 850 they began to build adobe and stone houses. Over time they connected these pueblos and enlarged them, and some of their structures accommodated more than a thousand residents. For example, the pueblos at Mesa Verde in Colorado may have housed more than 7,000 people. Again, like the Mogollon, the Anasazi retained pit houses for worship, a tradition that survives today. Some contemporary Pueblo still use sacred, semisubterranean rooms called *kivas.*

The definitive Anasazi apartment house was a huge semicircular complex that housed an entire village at Pueblo Bonito in New Mexico's Chaco Canyon. Constructed of stone with mud mortar and wooden beams, it had hundreds of rooms for its estimated 1,000 people. Pueblo Bonito was built about A.D. 920, serving as a major cultural center from which trade flowed to other settlements.

Scientists believe that as the population grew, the Anasazi migrated to the hinterlands. These multisatel-

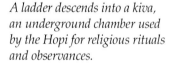

A ladder descends into a kiva, an underground chamber used by the Hopi for religious rituals and observances.

lite settlements were connected by an extensive road system. Although warfare may have been a factor, it appears that a long-lasting drought ultimately brought the great Anasazi culture to an end. Pueblo Bonito is a prime example of how alterations in the environment can bring a community to an end. The drought, possibly heightened by human activities, such as cutting the surrounding timber, exhausted the food supply. By A.D. 1300, most of the Anasazi communities were deserted.

Pueblo Bonito, the Anasazi village located in Chaco Canyon, New Mexico, was built around A.D. 920. At its peak, Pueblo Bonito was home to about 1,000 people.

Several Ojibwa tend to their daily chores at their camp on Lake Huron. Before the arrival of Europeans, American Indians had established sophisticated and diverse cultures throughout North America that were well adapted to the demands of their respective environments.

WHO ARE
THE AMERICAN
INDIANS?

Anthropologists have found the concept of culture areas helpful in classifying the original inhabitants of North America. A culture area may be defined as a region in which the people share certain cultural traits by virtue of their backgrounds and the environment. The peoples who lived in a given culture area usually had related languages, common religious beliefs, and similar kinds of economic, social, and political organization. Although the environment does not determine culture, it places important limits on the type of activities in which people can engage. For example, Native Americans in the far north could not become agriculturalists because of the climate. But they knew how to build shelters with blocks of snow, something southern Indians could not do.

Culture Areas

The culture area concept is useful in providing a general picture of Native Americans prior to the arrival of Europeans. When two or more peoples shared the same environment, they often devised similar behavioral patterns, such as how they hunted or what foods they grew and how they grew them. Yet they might be quite dissimilar in their political organization or in their kinship patterns. Scientists generally agree that prior to the arrival of Europeans there were 10 major culture areas in North America: Arctic, Subarctic, Northwest Coast, California, Plateau, Great Basin,

Southwest, Plains, Southeast, and Northeast–Great Lakes.

The character of a culture area often changed over time. It could, for example, become more diverse as new people with different customs moved into the region. Generalizations about an area are accurate for only a moment in time because cultural change is constant even without new arrivals. Also, the culture area concept should not be viewed as an accurate characterization of contemporary Native American life.

Arctic

The upper fringe of North America, extending from Alaska to Greenland along the edge of the Arctic Ocean, was (and continues to be) the home of the people often called the Eskimo, a corruption of an Indian word meaning "eaters of raw flesh." The people themselves prefer to be called the Inuit, meaning "the people" or "the human ones."

At the time of their first contact with Europeans, the Inuit varied somewhat in their physical nature from place to place. They tended to be relatively short, stocky,

An 1816 drawing depicts four Inuits from the Kotzebue Sound region in northwestern Alaska. The two Inuits in the middle are wearing ornamental lip plugs. To survive in the harsh environment of the Arctic, the Inuit hunted land and sea mammals and fished.

broad faced, and dark eyed. They had straight black head hair but little on the face or body. The Inuit also had a distinctive characteristic called the epicanthic fold, a fold of the skin of the upper eyelid over the inner angle or both angles of the eye. To survive in the harsh environment of snow and ice, the inhabitants of the Arctic culture area created a technology that allowed them to hunt land and sea mammals and to fish the ocean. Their prey served as more than just food. Animal hides, bones, and teeth were made into items for everyday living. Artisans created tools, ornaments, weapons, and masks of great beauty, and they were particularly skilled in carving ivory, bone, antler, stone, and wood.

Women were highly skilled in sewing, creating finely made waterproof clothing essential for life in the severe climate. Men were equally adept at making boats that gave them mobility at sea to hunt marine life. Their kayaks, made by stretching animal skins over a framework of driftwood, were designed to allow for the so-called kayak roll. When the boat capsized, it could be righted immediately. A strict division of labor placed reliance on both men and women for specialized skills, and survival depended on the cooperative efforts of the entire family. Dogs played an important role in transportation and in hunting by sniffing out seals beneath the ice and tracking game on land.

Because the Inuit needed to move about in their hunting activities, many did not establish settled villages. Those who lived near the sea were more sedentary. Although the Inuit are thought of as living in houses built of blocks of snow, that kind of shelter was usually temporary and used only during winter hunting. The Inuit in Alaska constructed semisubterranean, permanent homes using sod, wood, and even whalebone.

The Inuit held a number of secular and religious festivals. Their relationship with the supernatural was of great importance, and people governed their behavior by a series of taboos (social prohibitions). Spirits were thought of as both human and animal. Priests known as shamans served as intermediaries with the supernatural and as healers.

Subarctic

The Subarctic culture area, which spanned the entire North American continent from Alaska to Newfoundland, was composed of two main environments. The southern part of the region was a coniferous forest that extends over most of Canada and the interior of Alaska. The northern area, often called the Barren Grounds, was cold and bleak. The people who occupied this region spoke dialects of two great language groups, Algonquian and Athapaskan. In the east from Hudson Bay to Labrador, the Cree, Ojibwa, Naskapi, and other tribes were Algonquian speakers. To the west and north, Athapaskan tongues were spoken by the Chipewayan and by tribes such as the Slave, Yellowknife, Dogrib, Hare, and Kutchin.

The peoples of the Subarctic culture area moved frequently to sustain life by hunting and fishing in the numerous lakes of the southeastern region. They usually traveled in family bands, transporting their belongings on toboggans when possible and camping wherever food was to be found. In warmer weather, they moved over lakes and streams in lightweight birch-bark canoes, which were easily portable. Birch bark was also made into containers and used as a covering for shelters.

The people's quest for food never ended. They fished and hunted waterfowl, caribou, moose, bear, and smaller mammals. Enormous caribou herds migrated seasonally and not only provided food but clothing and shelter as well. Sinew was used to fashion hides into moccasins, leggings, mittens, tunics, and tipi coverings, and strips of rawhide were used in the manufacture of snowshoes, sleds, and toboggans.

The Ojibwa—who lived in the area of present-day Ontario, Minnesota, northern Wisconsin, and Michigan—did not follow caribou herds like other northern tribes. Instead, they relied upon less migratory game animals that lived in the heavily forested region. In the spring, the Ojibwa made sugar from maple tree sap, and at the end of summer they harvested a grain Europeans called "wild rice," which was a misnomer because considerable cultivation was involved. This adequate food supply enabled the Ojibwa to lead a more settled way of life.

Among the Ojibwa, Cree, and some other eastern groups, the Grand Medicine Society, or Midewiwin, was a vital religious institution. The Midewiwin consisted of men and women who were healers. One of the Athapaskan's supernatural beliefs was that spirits lived in the water and on the land and were embodied in the animals they sought for food. A special rapport with the spirit world was maintained by shamans who either inherited their powers or secured them through dreams. Shamans both cured patients with prayer and herbal remedies and used magic to control spirits.

Northwest Coast

The Northwest Coast culture area extended more than 2,000 miles from northern California to southern Alaska and included present-day Oregon, Washington, and British Columbia. Some of the principal groups that lived in this area prior to the arrival of Europeans were the Tlingit, Haida, Tsimshian, Bella Coola, Makah, Kwakiutl, Cowichan, and Chinook.

The temperate, rainy climate of the Northwest Coast provided the people of the region with a far more abundant and constant food supply than was available to their neighbors in the Arctic and Subarctic. They gathered berries and other forest products, fished the rivers, and exploited the bounty of the sea with great skill. Some groups hunted the whale, and most sought the sea otter, which yielded one of the most beautiful furs in the world. They traded extensively among themselves as well as with inland groups. Some groups made voyages of several days' duration in their beautifully formed canoes.

Northwest Coast groups formed affluent and highly complex societies. They generally lived in established villages in winter, which was a time for traditional festivities. Usually villages were arranged along a riverbank or an estuary set back from the ocean. Houses were occupied by groups of relatives rather than a single nuclear family. A chief's house served as a residence not only for his relatives but also for his slaves and other nonrelated persons.

The village was the primary social unit with limited tribal organization. Society was stratified with chiefs and nobles at the top, commoners beneath them, and slaves occupying the lowest echelon. In summer, the people frequently changed their residence to be near their favorite fishing and hunting spots. Some tribes followed a form of *matrilineal descent* (tracing descent through the mother's family), whereas others were *patrilineal* (tracing descent through the father's family). Clan lineages were associated with animals (totems) such as ravens, eagles, beavers, and bears. These creatures were mythological heroes and were featured as elements on totem poles, which portrayed legendary clan histories.

Little is known about the religion of the Northwest Coast peoples. In the north, it is believed to have been an individual affair, with a shaman serving as an intermediary between humans and the spirit world. Among the Kwakiutl, religion was more formalized, with the existence of secret societies. Their ceremonies featured dancing and singing. Performers wore elaborate regalia, including headdresses and masks of great beauty. Masks portrayed both humans and animals, and some were intricately formed with moving parts. *Potlatches* were ceremonial feasts that lasted several days and to which hundreds of guests were invited. The host validated his rank by providing his guests with great quantities of food and gifts.

Northwest Coast artistic creations in wood, bone, and ivory were among the finest in all of North America, a tradition that continues today. Men worked native copper into ornaments, knives, and plaques—all of which were important symbols of wealth. Women produced fine baskets and wove decorated blankets of cedar bark mixed with mountain-goat or dog hair.

California

The California culture area, bounded on the east by the Sierra Nevada and on the west by the Pacific Ocean, was home to more than 100 distinct tribes and sub-tribes that spoke numerous dialects from 6 different language families. The great linguistic diversity in the area can be attributed to the isolation of some groups and the influx of many new peoples who migrated to the region. Some of the larger tribes that lived in the area were the Pomo, Miwok, Chumash, Luiseño, and Cahuilla. Generally, people in the California culture area enjoyed an abundance of food and a mild climate, except for those who lived in the harsher desert areas of the south.

The family was the basis of social life. Small villages were formed of several male-related families. Men, who inherited their roles, provided village leadership, but their power was slight. Their homes and modes of dress were the same as other villagers. Religious beliefs and practices varied but tended to emphasize origin myths, supernatural spirits, and shamanism. Some groups had shamans who were primarily concerned with healing. Women served as shamans in some groups, such as the Hupa.

Some of the Chumash were seagoing people who lived on the mainland and on the Channel Islands off Santa Barbara. Adept boatmen, they scoured the off-

shore kelp beds for fish and also caught sea mammals. On the other hand, the Pomo (like most other California Indians) relied heavily on acorns. Harvested in the fall, the nuts were dried, hulled, and ground into a type of flour that had to be leached to rid it of bitter tannic acid before it was edible. The Pomo are distinguished for their excellent baskets, perhaps the finest in America.

California had certain natural products that were in great demand. One was salt. Another was obsidian, a stone that was unsurpassed for such things as arrowheads and cutting tools. Most California groups traded with their neighbors, exchanging their surpluses for things they lacked. Acorns, seaweed, canoes, salt,

This painting depicts the village life of California Indians. The villagers engage in various chores, including cracking acorns to make flour, rolling out dough to make bread, and starting a fire. The California culture area was home to more than 100 tribes that spoke a wide variety of languages.

dried fish, obsidian, weapons, cordage, and furs were among the items bartered.

Plateau

Bracketed between the Cascade Range in the west and the Rockies in the east is the high plateau region through which the Frazer and Columbia rivers wind. The people of this region relied heavily on the fish in these two rivers and their tributaries for food. Reaching down from inland British Columbia, the Plateau culture area covered portions of present-day Montana, Idaho, Washington, Oregon, and small sections of California and Wyoming.

The way of life of the Plateau Indians was a composite drawn from Indian cultures of the neighboring culture areas: Northwest Coast, California, Great Basin,

Plateau region Indians paddle their canoe along the Columbia River. The rivers in the Plateau culture area served as transportation routes for traders who carried goods from the interior of the continent to the Pacific Coast.

Plains, and Subarctic. Over thousands of years, peoples migrating into this region brought new languages and customs with them, resulting in even greater diversity despite a fairly constant environment. The Nez Percé, Cayuse, Klamath, Klikitat, Walla Walla, and Umatilla are thought to have been descendants of peoples who spoke Penutian languages and who came to the region about 6000 B.C. In the north, in eastern Washington and British Columbia, the people were Interior Salish speakers. They entered the Plateau area around 1500 B.C. Among the tribes descended from them are the Flathead, Spokane, Coeur d'Alene, Kalispel, and Columbia Indians.

Prior to the arrival of the Europeans, some 100,000 people lived in the Plateau region. No major political confederations arose among them. Self-sufficient communities, usually located along riverbanks, were governed by hereditary headmen who exercised limited power. The people fished, relying on salmon in particular, and gathered wild onions, carrots, nuts, and berries. The camas bulb, the starchy root of a type of lily, was an important food source, and the diet was augmented by hunting deer, mountain sheep, elk, and rabbits. People lived in flimsy, mat-covered windbreaks during summer. More substantial semisubterranean houses, made of logs and earth, or tentlike lodges provided shelter in winter.

The rivers, particularly the Columbia, served as transportation routes for traders. The Chinook came from the Pacific Coast, bringing salmon, sea otter pelts, and shells, which they exchanged for deerskins, bitterroot, and raw materials for making baskets. Trade introduced a significant new element in the 18th century when horses were brought in from the Plains and the Great Basin.

Descendants of horses first brought by the Spaniards to Mexico flourished in the New World. The Yakima and the Nez Percé developed huge herds of horses on their grasslands. The horse enabled the

Plateau People to range as far as California and the Plains to trade. The Flathead, Kutenai, and especially the Nez Percé adopted not only a wide range of Plains culture elements relating to the horse but also clothing and housing styles. European weapons and beads came into the hands of Plateau People via trade long before the Europeans themselves arrived. Unfortunately, the native traders from the coast also carried with them devastating foreign diseases such as smallpox, measles, and typhus.

Great Basin

Composed mostly of the states of Nevada and Utah, the enormous western desert known as the Great Basin includes western Colorado, southern Idaho, and corners of Oregon and Wyoming. Bounded by the Snake River in the north, the withered land sweeps south to the Mojave Desert. The sun-parched earth runs on mile after desolate mile, and clumps of sagebrush, cactus, and greasewood bushes dot the thirsty landscape. Within this area lived such groups as the Shoshone, Northern and Southern Paiute, and Washoe.

Over thousands of years, these peoples and their ancestors perceived that life in the desert could be sustained but it was a constant battle. Their search for food and water was never ending; there were seasonal differences and patterns that made survival possible. Small hunting parties of related individuals sought seeds, berries, roots, insects, snakes, lizards, and rodents. In the foothills of the surrounding mountains, piñon nuts could be found. Streams fed by melting snows and upland rains provided water, and sometimes there were fish in the streams. Larger mammals were scarce, but rabbits provided both food and clothing. Their skins were sewn together to make robes for chilly weather, but most of the time clothing and footgear were not worn. Because people moved about constantly, they relied on simple shelters that were abandoned and reproduced over and over again.

Great Basin society was essentially egalitarian. Political and social organization was simple—the small family foraging units required little more than the wisdom of an elder. Life in this resource-poor region was precarious at best. Women played an important role in a family's survival because they were the primary gatherers. Preparing and cooking the plants from the desert's meager supply was difficult. Piñon nuts were ground into flour, providing an important staple. Women also served as shamans, who were primarily healers. Their powers were believed to be derived from animal spirits that appeared to them in dreams. Shamans also had extensive knowledge of countless plants, such as cinnabar and mentzelia seeds, which were used to treat ailments.

Southwest

The Southwest culture area corresponded roughly to present-day Arizona and New Mexico and extended along the Rio Grande into Texas. Some of the best-known Native Americans—the Hopi, Navajo, Apache, and Pueblo—lived (and still live) in the region. It is a dry land of flat open spaces, deep canyons carved out of stone by the timeless wash of rivers, and of rugged, pine-cloaked mountains.

The Hopi built villages, consisting of stone houses plastered with mud, that were situated atop mesas hundreds of feet above the flatlands where their crops were grown. The elevation, although inconvenient, was a form of defense from hostile tribes that raided the region. The Hopi made their way back and forth along steep, narrow trails over the face of the cliff. Although there was little water for irrigation, the Hopi successfully grew the same plants they had for centuries: corn, squash, beans, and tobacco. One of the oldest Hopi pueblos, Oraibi on Black Mesa, has been occupied for 1,000 years.

The Hopi were a deeply religious people who valued peace and ritual over war. A central feature of their pueblos were the kivas, underground chambers that were used for religious observances and as men's clubhouses. Kivas were entered through a hole in the roof by a ladder and served as symbols of the spirit underworld, the place that the Hopi believed (and some continue to believe) human souls returned to after death. The spirits of the World Below were called *kachinas*, which were thought to be all-powerful, capable of bringing rain and assuring good harvests. Ritual life for the Hopi was rich and demanding, often involving the entire pueblo. Among the Hopi the terms *chief* and *priest* were virtually interchangeable, which was true of many Indian groups.

The people who settled near the Hopi in the 15th century were the Navajo. They called themselves the Dineh, which means "the people." Their language was Athapaskan, and scholars believe that they moved south from northwestern Canada. The Navajo were originally hunters, but they learned to be farmers and, subsequently, herders of sheep. After settling in the Southwest, the Navajo borrowed many things from their neighbors: new crafts, skills, and even mythological beliefs. Like the Hopi, the Navajo were deeply religious. They had elaborate curing ceremonies, one of which incorporated the creation of intricate designs by sprinkling ground-up minerals and vegetable materials on a smooth bed of sand. These so-called sand paintings are uniquely Navajo. The people lived in conical or multisided houses called *hogans*, which were made of logs and mud on level ground.

The Apache lived east and south of the Hopi and Navajo. Like the Navajo, they were Athapaskan speakers who are believed to have come from the same area in Canada about 500 years ago. Initially, both the Apache and the Navajo raided other groups, but the

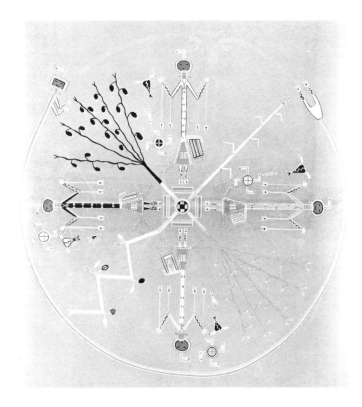

The Navajo have traditionally created beautifully colored sandpaintings, such as the Mountain Chant, that they use in healing rituals. In producing sandpaintings, artists trickle finely ground sand and mineral pigments through their fingers onto the ground. The symbolic powers of sandpaintings are used to cure the sick and are then destroyed at the end of the ritual.

Apache continued to pillage and became widely feared as ruthless warriors. The Apache tribes shared a common cultural base and language; nevertheless, they came to take on different cultural characteristics, depending on their location. The Jicarilla Apache of northern New Mexico, for example, were influenced by the Plains peoples, and the group that joined with the Plains Kiowa became known as Kiowa Apache and followed some Kiowa ways. None of the Apache had any central tribal organization. Bands composed of extended family groups followed a headman, perhaps a warrior of some importance. Apache housing was simple: a pole framework covered with brush.

Two other groups, the Pima and Papago, were farming tribes descended from the ancient Hohokam People. The Papago were seminomadic, whereas the Pima were a settled people who used irrigation to grow their crops. The Pima had a more complex social and political organization, with both village and tribal chiefs. Both tribes had patrilineal clans and worshiped the same deities.

Plains

The central grasslands of North America sweep southward from Saskatchewan and Alberta in Canada to Texas, bounded on the west by the Rockies and extending east as far as Minnesota, Iowa, Missouri, and Arkansas. On this predominantly treeless grassland lived tribes who have come to represent the romanticized view of the Indian warriors and hunters as bronze-skinned horsemen, with their feathered headdresses streaming in the wind, galloping across the prairie in pursuit of buffalo or raiding enemy camps. The Sioux, Blackfeet, Cheyenne, Kiowa, and Comanche, among others, whose way of life inspired the stereotype, were actually very late arrivals in the area. For centuries their predecessors, small nomadic bands of hunters, had maintained a marginal existence. By A.D. 1000, some groups were engaged in farming along the Missouri River, but drought drove most of them away shortly afterward.

The Plains region, like California, had many migrations into and through it. Around 1300, groups began to invade the territory from all directions. They came as village dwellers who survived in the environment by mixing agriculture with hunting and gathering. The first group may have been the Pawnee, who migrated to Nebraska from Texas. They were followed by the Wichita, and later on such tribes as the Mandan, Hidatsa, Assiniboin, Crow, Dakota, Omaha, and Osage moved into the region from the east. The Mandan became growers of corn and lived in large established villages. Some later migrants were driven to the region because of aggressive tribes such as the Iroquois. From the west came the Comanche and Kiowa.

Because the native American horse had become extinct, Indians had no knowledge of such an animal until after European contact. The Spanish explorer Francisco Vásquez de Coronado had horses with him when his expedition visited the Plains in 1541, but that was 200 years before Indians came to possess them in significant numbers. As early as the 17th century, some Plains groups had begun to secure horses through trade or raids on Indian groups to the south who already possessed them. The Comanche and Crow were noted horsemen and breeders.

The Indians of the Plains had been traders long before the arrival of whites. In the Plains (as in many other culture areas), foreign goods, metal tools, woven cloth, glass beads, and guns preceded the arrival of Europeans. These new items, especially horses and guns, had a major impact on Plains culture. Baggage once loaded on poles and pulled by dogs could be

Comanche drive a herd of buffalo toward a cliff ledge. Plains Indians sometimes organized communal hunts in which they would kill a large number of buffalo by driving an entire herd over a cliff or into an enclosure where they could easily kill the trapped animals.

hauled more easily by horses. The conical tipi so identified with Plains peoples was first developed in the northern forests by groups who covered a framework of poles with birch bark or hides. The Plains residents adapted these portable dwellings to their requirements. The tipi poles were lashed to a horse, which could drag much larger loads and travel twice as far in a day's time than a dog could.

Buffalo were a major source of food, and they also supplied many other requirements. Their hides provided warm robes, storage containers, and tipi coverings and served as canvases for paintings that were records of important events. A host of additional needs were met by buffalo hair, sinew, horns, and bone. With the introduction of the horse, many sedentary peoples adopted a more nomadic way of life that centered on hunting the buffalo. The Mandan and Hidatsa, who lived along the Missouri River in the Dakotas, also hunted buffalo but remained agriculturalists and did not become nomadic.

So effective were horses (and subsequently horses and guns) in the quest for buffalo that the time required to hunt them was greatly reduced. This allowed opportunities for other activities, such as warfare, which Indians pursued to secure more horses and hunting territory. In the process, a warrior could greatly enhance his prestige by acts of bravery. Plains culture reached its peak with the coming of the horse but ended after only a century with the overwhelming advance of whites.

Although the Plains Indians adapted new material things, they were reluctant to give up their supernatural beliefs. Their religions emphasized the powers of nature: the sun, sky, land, water, and animals. Wolves, bears, beavers, and elk were animals whose spirits were particularly involved in the conferring of power. By depriving themselves of food and water while in isolation, young men sought visions in which some of an animal's power might be transferred to them. Those who obtained power from the same animal formed cults that honored that spirit. An especially important Plains Indian ceremony was the Sun Dance, a complex ritual that involved great personal pain for the participant. Such suffering and endurance not only provided a link to the Great Spirit but also affirmed one's identity.

Southeast

The Southeast culture area extended from the Atlantic Ocean to east Texas and from the Gulf of Mexico to the Mississippi and Ohio valleys. The region was primarily wooded, and animal life was abundant in the forests. Deer were sought in particular. Small game was hunted with blowguns. Women grew such crops as corn, squash, pumpkins, and tobacco after men cleared the land. The area also had a rich soil that provided ample harvests to sustain life. In subsequent centuries, colonists would eagerly covet this agricultural domain and accelerate the process of expelling Indians from their lands.

There was a common cultural core between such groups as the Seminole, Cherokee, Creek, Choctaw, Chickasaw, and Natchez, but the peoples had many different languages. Communities were organized into matrilineal clans. This cultural feature is often found in societies where women are agriculturalists and provide the main food supply. Women also wove baskets and mats, made pottery, and tanned hides. People needed little clothing, donning only skin robes or turkey-feather cloaks in cooler weather.

Most of the people made homes along river valleys and organized into villages. The people lived in villages with palisades for protection against enemies. Earthen-floored houses were made of supporting poles covered with saplings, mud, and grass. Villages usually had a playing field and several structures for council meetings. Chiefs led more by example and precept than by

Several Creek enjoy a leisurely moment outside their house. The man in the foreground smokes tobacco in a long pipe. Many early Indian groups considered tobacco a sacred crop, and pipe smoking became an integral part of rituals surrounding war, peace, harvest, and death throughout North America, particularly in the Southeast culture area.

force. The village councils, composed of warriors, considered matters of importance and strove for consensus among their members.

Tobacco was a sacred crop. It is not known where or when it was first grown, but it may have originated in Mexico. Tobacco pipes, which were also used for smoking grasses and other plants, have been found in the Southeast dating to 1590 B.C., but identifiable traces of tobacco itself only date to about A.D. 1000. Hopewell burial mounds frequently contained carved effigy pipes. Because the Hopewell People were a cultural force that extended from Florida to Canada, it is not surprising that such a trait was incorporated into the ceremonial practices of other regions. Pipe smoking—an important ritual associated with funerals, peace overtures, and healing—was a widespread cultural practice throughout many parts of North America. By the time Europeans arrived, tobacco was a valued trade item of Native Americans, and it become a major export item of the early colonists.

Northeast–Great Lakes

The Northeast–Great Lakes culture area was bounded by the Mississippi River on the west, the Great Lakes and the St. Lawrence River on the north, the Atlantic Ocean on the east, and present-day North Carolina on the south. At the time Europeans began to arrive in the 17th century, it was the home of such diverse groups as the Abenaki, Penobscot, Narraganset, Pequot, Delaware, Powhatan, Huron, Algonquian, Shawnee, Illinois, and Winnebago. The Mohawk, Oneida, Onondaga, Cayuga, Seneca, and Tuscarora—six tribes that are often referred to as the Iroquois—also lived in this region. The majority of these people were Algonquian speakers, but in parts of the Atlantic Coast region and in a pocket east of the Great Lakes, Iroquoian-speaking peoples held sway. In the far west, the Winnebago spoke a Siouan tongue.

The Northeast–Great Lakes culture area varied greatly in its environment, which resulted in great differences in life-styles among groups. The western portion of the area was a transitional zone that encompassed the eastern prairie, whereas the region to the east was heavily wooded. Indeed, the people of the territory are often referred to as the Woodland Indians. The hardwood forests were filled with game, and the many trees provided raw materials for shelter, tools, and fuel. Forest animals were the primary food source. People also took advantage of the abundant marine life along the Atlantic shore and fished the inland rivers and lakes. Like tribes elsewhere in the region, except in the northern areas where it was too cold for much agriculture, the Great Lakes peoples relied upon farming and hunting.

The people in the northern region were mostly seminomadic hunters who needed portable shelters such as hide-covered tents or bark-covered wigwams. In the north, moose hides were used to make clothing that was decorated with porcupine quills, shells, and feathers. In most other areas, deerskin clothing was worn, much of it decorated with floral designs created first with dyed porcupine quills and later, after contact with Europeans, with glass trade beads.

Throughout the Northeast, villages were usually situated near a river, stream, or lake and surrounded by garden plots in which corn, pumpkins, and beans were grown. When the soil became depleted, new plots were cleared by cutting and burning trees and underbrush. Houses were generally of two types: rectangular, bark-covered longhouses with barrel-shaped roofs and wigwams with bent or straight pole frames covered with mats, bark, or skins. Villages were usually surrounded by palisades, as in the Southeast culture area. Tribes frequently raided each other, seeking revenge, glory, or property. Disputes over hunting grounds often resulted in fighting. Hand weapons such as the tomahawk, spear, and bow and arrow were commonly used.

Religious beliefs incorporated the concept of a Supreme Being to whom prayers were directed and with whom contact was sought through dreams. The Mohawk believed in a spiritual force, *orenda*, which was present in all things, including humans. Many people conceived of an afterlife, and objects were buried with the dead to serve their needs there. Shamans served as intermediaries with the spirit world.

Perhaps the best-known people of this culture area were the Iroquois tribes of Central New York—the Mohawk, Oneida, Onondaga, Cayuga, and Seneca— who formed a confederacy called the Five Nations or the League of the Iroquois before the arrival of Europeans. After the Tuscaroras were driven out of their homeland on the Atlantic Coast by Europeans in the early 1700s, they joined the Iroquois. Thereafter, the league was referred to as the Six Nations. Each year, the Grand Council of the league, with delegations from all the tribes, met at Onondaga, the foremost village of that tribe. Although peace chiefs called *sachems* occupied the council seats, they were appointed and could be removed by tribal matriarchs who monitored their actions. Iroquois society was organized around matrilineal families, lineages, and clans. Some contemporary Iroquois believe that several aspects of their society were incorporated by the Founding Fathers into the Constitution of the new American nation. They are quick to point out ways in which they were more democratic than the citizens of ancient Rome and Greece. The domain of the Iroquois stretched from New England to Illinois, an area larger than many European kingdoms.

Fundamental to Iroquois life was the longhouse, a multifamily, arch-roofed, rectangular dwelling from 50 to 150 feet in length that was constructed of elm poles and bark. A longitudinal corridor allowed passage within the house, and small fires for cooking, light, and warmth burned at intervals along its course. On either side of the corridor were platforms for sleeping and storage, arranged in family compartments.

Tobacco was one of the most important crops among the Great Lakes People, and it had tremendous religious significance. The plant was thought to be a gift from the spirits, and it was often used to propitiate them. Here the all-pervasive spirit called orenda among other groups was known as *manitou*. The Iroquois believed that spirits infused everything. Some, like the False Faces, were malevolent and could cause disease. Members of a religious group named the False Face Society wore frightening masks that held curative powers.

English explorer Henry Hudson trades with Indians along the river in New York that is named after him. Hudson was one of the many Europeans who came to the New World in search of a Northwest Passage to the Pacific Ocean. From the 16th century to the 18th century, expeditions from England, Portugal, France, Spain, and Holland unsuccessfully sought the elusive passage. Most of these expeditions resulted in some type of contact with Native Americans.

STRANGERS ARRIVE

The peoples and cultures of North America were devastatingly changed by contact with Europeans. Following the tradition of the day, explorers in the service of Spain, Great Britain, France, Russia, and Holland claimed sovereignty over portions of the continent for the European powers. It was irrelevant to Europe's rulers that millions of native peoples throughout North America had long governed themselves under their own political systems. The emergence of the United States as an independent nation in 1776 further affected Native American peoples and cultures.

Although any short answer to the question of why the European intruders triumphed over the indigenous populations of North America would be simplistic, two prime reasons have often been cited: weaponry and disease. Initial relationships between native peoples and foreigners were often friendly. When hostilities arose, however, the superior military hardware of the Europeans almost always prevailed. The offshore vessel with cannons, the mounted soldier with a sword, or a cadre of troops armed with muskets proved formidable weapons against spears, clubs, and bows and arrows. But in the end, disease killed more Native Americans than warfare.

Scientists differ greatly in their estimates of the native population of the New World at the time of Christopher Columbus's arrival in 1492, but they calculate that the population was probably somewhere between 13 and 33 million. From the time of initial contact, populations declined rapidly as Indians were exposed to Old World diseases against which they had no immunity. Although Europeans were not completely immune, they had developed antibodies that helped fight off many sicknesses that proved fatal to Indians. For example, a sailor with measles might only feel slightly ill as he came ashore, but the natives he encountered, having lived in isolation and never having been exposed to measles, were highly susceptible. Catastrophic epidemics swept through Indian villages; among them were smallpox, measles, whooping cough, chicken pox, bubonic plague, typhus, diphtheria, amoebic dysentery, influenza, and perhaps malaria. Historians agree that there was massive native mortality, possibly as much as 90 percent of the population.

The young and the old usually died in the greatest numbers. A group's religious and cultural knowledge was lost with the death of elders, and some diseases affected the ability of women to reproduce or carry a baby to term, thereby directly affecting the size of future populations. Over time, general health deteriorated as a result of insufficient food and the introduction of alcohol by the Europeans. By the end of the 19th century, some observers believed that Native Americans might become extinct because their numbers had declined so radically.

The First Europeans Arrive

Christopher Columbus, an Italian sailing in the service of Spain, has traditionally been credited with being the first European to sight the New World in 1492. However, during the exploration of Greenland, Erik raude Thorvaldsson (Erik the Red) and other Norsemen made a number of landfalls in North America more than 900 years ago. L'Anse aux Meadows, an archaeological site on the northern tip of Newfoundland, attests to the existence of a small non-Indian colony dating to approximately A.D. 1000. Archaeologists have uncovered house foundations and a smithy containing numerous iron boat rivets. It is not known what became of these first colonists or, indeed, who they actually were, but Vikings did settle Greenland, and Norse sagas describe four expeditions to the North American coast, including a confrontation with the natives on the coast of Labrador in 1003.

John Cabot, an Italian in the service of Britain, sighted North America in 1497, believing it was China. Like Columbus, Cabot was seeking a northern route to Asia when he sighted Nova Scotia and Newfoundland. His landfall marked the beginning of the end for the Beothuk, a small tribe that lived on the island. In the centuries that followed, the Beothuk were systematically enslaved or hunted and killed by Europeans, and by the 1800s they had become extinct as a cultural group.

Spain sent forth a series of ships to claim and conquer the New World. Juan Ponce de León, who had sailed under Columbus, explored the islands that were to be named Puerto Rico and the Bahamas, and he sighted Florida in 1513. Hernán Cortés, Álvar Núñez Cabeza de Vaca, and Pánfilo de Narváez, among others, carried Spain's flag to various parts of North and South America during the early 1500s.

Not to be outdone by Spain, France sent its own explorers to the Atlantic Coast of North America. Giovanni da Verrazano, an Italian sailing under the French flag, sighted New York and Narragansett Bay in 1524. Ten years later, Jacques Cartier, in search of a passage to the Pacific Ocean, is credited with being the first European to explore the Saint Lawrence River. He

Explorer Jacques Cartier raises a cross in present-day Canada to claim the territory for France. The French established settlements in Canada to expand the fur trade but found the area less suitable for agriculture than the regions to the south that were occupied by the British.

encountered friendly Indians who eagerly traded with the Europeans. On his second exploration (1535–36), he entered the Huron village called Hochelaga, which later became the important French stronghold of Montreal. Cartier's third effort (1541–43) was considered a failure; he discovered no Northwest passage, and his gold and diamonds turned out to be pyrites and quartz.

In 1539, after experiences in Central America, Spain's Hernando de Soto led an exploration through Florida, Georgia, and Alabama to the Mississippi River, leaving death and destruction in his wake. Francisco Vásquez de Coronado in 1540 began his own journey through Mexico into the Southwest. In 1542, Spanish ships sailing north from Mexico on a voyage of exploration encountered Chumash Indians off the coast of California. Spain established its first North American settlement at Saint Augustine, Florida, in 1565, and the Spaniards later had a significant impact on Indians in California and the Southwest.

Following the pattern of colonization it established in Central and South America, Spain sent administrators, soldiers, and priests to plunder the natural resources of North America and subdue its native populations. Spanish adventurers, mostly men who aspired to nobility and who called themselves *conquistadores* (conquerors), came to the New World in search of fame and fortune. Priests, who came to extend Christianity to the west, demanded that native people convert to their religion in order that their soul might be saved. Both groups came to be feared by the Indians. Some settlers also came to the New World. Frequently, they had received large ranches, including slaves from the native population, as a reward for their previous service to the Spanish crown.

Martin Frobisher began a new British era of exploration in 1576. He encountered the Inuit on Greenland and Baffin Island. John Davis, Henry Hudson, Sir Thomas Button, Robert Bylot, and Luke Fox continued explorations for the next six decades, providing extensive knowledge of Baffin and Hudson bays.

French interest in North America rekindled in the 1580s, when the export of furs proved profitable. In 1603, Samuel de Champlain explored inland to determine possible locations for settlements. Champlain established Quebec as an important post, and he formed a strong alliance with the Huron to obtain furs. Champlain's Huron allies encouraged him to attack their traditional foes, the Iroquois, who then became united against the French. Champlain was even wounded in one raid and would have died if he had not been carried to safety by his Indian allies.

For a time the Huron prevailed against their enemies, but the Iroquois fought back more successfully once they secured arms from Dutch traders in New York. Ultimately, the Iroquois killed or chased the Huron off their lands. The Iroquois also perceived advantages to be had through an alignment with Great Britain, and the 17th century became a time of conflict between the French and the Iroquois. French troops finally suppressed the Iroquois and established Iroquois neutrality by treaty.

France sent many missionaries to North America, including the Jesuits, who established their first permanent mission among the western Huron in 1634. Although the Jesuits actively attempted to Christianize the Indians and teach them French ways, they demonstrated a far greater tolerance for native culture than did Spanish missionaries. France continued to send its explorers inland. One of the most notable adventurers was René-Robert Cavelier, Sieur de La Salle, whose party descended the Mississippi River to the Gulf of Mexico. He claimed the vast territory through which he passed for France, naming it Louisiana after King Louis XIV.

Spain had ignored the Southwest for 40 years after Coronado's expedition. But in 1598, Don Juan de Oñate took control of what is presently New Mexico, where a number of missions were established. Oñate's legacy as governor was one of death and destruction. Indians who resisted the Spanish were treated harshly. After decades of mistreatment, the Pueblo Rebellion erupted in 1680. Led by a San Juan Pueblo medicine man named Popé, the Indians surprised the Spanish, killing hundreds of them. They burned the mission churches and ranches and expelled the Spanish from their provincial capital in Santa Fe. Popé restored the native customs and religion, eliminating Spanish-Christian influences. This was atypical for the peaceful Hopi, but their insurrection clearly indicated their attitude toward Spanish domination. Spanish rule was reestablished when Popé died in 1692.

Spanish contact with Indians remained inconsequential until the middle of the 18th century, when Spain began to fear that either Russia or England, both of which had claimed part of the Pacific Coast, would

(continued on page 73)

A CULTURAL
REJUVENATION

Overleaf: *Dressed in ceremonial costumes, a group of young Indians prepares for a dance competition at a powwow (Indian get-together) in Tulsa, Oklahoma. Intertribal powwows are held regularly, providing Native Americans with the opportunity to perform traditional dances and songs and to exchange and preserve cultural information.*

Indians have a rich legacy in the arts, and the works of Native American painters, potters, sculptors, weavers, and silversmiths are highly valued by commercial galleries, museums, and collectors. Opposite page: Using his expertise in beadwork, a Sioux craftsman creates a wide array of ceremonial and decorative items. Above: Sioux quilt makers display their bedcovers at a powwow. Left: Using a vertical loom, a Navajo weaves a blanket with traditional designs.

Many Indians today work hard to sustain their tribes, influence public policy, and represent their people. *Opposite page: Wilma Mankiller has served as the principal chief of the Cherokee Nation of Oklahoma since 1985.* **Above:** *Enoch Kelly Haney, Oklahoma state senator and artist, stands in front of one of his paintings.* Right: *Arbo Mikkanen, a Kiowa, is a law student at the University of Oklahoma.*

Indians actively seek to protect tribal resources and preserve their culture. Above: *In July 1986, a group of Navajo march through their reservation in Arizona in a show of solidarity against the impending removal of some tribe members from their land. The federal government had previously announced plans to transfer some tracts of land from the Navajo reservation to the Hopi reservation.* Opposite page: *In Plymouth, Massachusetts, Indians from the Wampanoag, Mohawk, and Micmac nations, among others, beat a drum in a unifying ceremony during a day of mourning on Thanksgiving Day, 1986. One of the purposes of the day of mourning was to shatter the public's idealized image of the pilgrims.*

A Navajo watches over a herd of sheep in Monument Valley, Arizona. Indians remain proud bearers of their culture, and their Native American heritage often is expressed in their everyday life. Today, most Indians live within two cultures—one native and traditional, the other Western.

(continued from page 64)

contest its claim to California. Spain sent soldiers and missionaries to solidify its hold over the Pacific region and its people. The first Spanish mission was established in California in 1769. Others were added and the mission period lasted for the next 65 years. Many contemporary Indians consider that period a time of slavery. Spanish influence and domination continued to the south in Mexico, which did not win its freedom from Spain until 1821.

The Dutch and English in the East

Through the efforts of Henry Hudson, a British captain in the employ of the Dutch East India Company, Holland claimed portions of the mid-Atlantic region. In 1609, Hudson sailed up the river named for him in search of the fabled passage to Asia but instead found Mahican and Wappinger tribes. Later, one of the most famous purchases in the world occurred in 1626, when

Isaac Jogues, a French Jesuit missionary, preaches to a group of Mohawk. Jogues, who served as an ambassador of peace to the Mohawk, was killed by a hostile member of that tribe in 1646. Jogues was canonized in 1930 as one of the Jesuit Martyrs of North America. France sent many missionaries to North America to Christianize the Indians and instruct them in European customs.

Peter Minuit (holding scroll), director-general of the Dutch West India Company's North American settlements, buys the island of Manhattan from Indians in 1626 for merchandise valued at 60 guilders (later estimated to be worth $24). Dutch control over the region ended when the British captured Dutch settlements in the 1670s.

the Dutch bought the island of Manhattan for beads and trinkets reportedly worth $24. The Dutch soon entered into the fur trade, but their commercial activities were short-lived because the British captured New Amsterdam (New York) and Fort Orange (Albany) in the 1670s. Dutch settlers who had established profitable farms and estates remained and merged with the British colonists.

In 1670, Great Britain granted a charter to the Hudson's Bay Company, empowering it to seek a northwest passage, to occupy lands adjacent to Hudson Bay, and to conduct commerce. The company offered guns, gunpowder, metal tools and utensils, and wool blankets to Indians in exchange for fur pelts. And later on, when further inducement was needed, alcohol became the stimulus for trade.

British explorers, along with the French and Dutch, found no precious jewels, but they did find magnificent fur-bearing animals that had great economic value. Pelts became the principal export from North America. Indians had previously relied on hunting for subsistence and, in a minor way, on trade with other tribes. The commercial trapping of fur-bearing animals ended their centuries-old patterns of seasonal migration, and the dependence on new foods and European goods induced some native people to settle near trading posts. The posts became convenient places for the women and children to stay while the men embarked on extended journeys in quest of pelts, particularly those of the beaver, whose fur was used in the manufacture of hats popular in Europe.

The fur trade established a life-style that was exceptionally detrimental to the Indian way of life, especially through the exchange of guns and alcohol for pelts. At times, some trading companies sought to ban the sale of guns, but there were always other foreign traders prepared to deal in them. Warfare that had once been fought with tomahawks, spears, and bows and arrows became more deadly, and disputes were often uneven because not all tribes had access to the same weaponry. Armed tribes raided the villages of other Indians and sometimes seized their territories, forcing defeated tribes to move to new regions.

The Jamestown Settlement

The first British settlements in North America were failures with the exception of Jamestown, Virginia. Founded in 1607 by Captain John Smith, Jamestown was ultimately a success for the settlers, and it proved to be pivotal for the Indians of the Tidewater region. The Jamestown settlement presents a typical picture of the effects of the contact between Indians and colonists on the eastern seaboard in the 17th century. The day-to-day activities of the community were under the direction of John Rolfe, who is well known in American folklore for marrying Chief Powhatan's daughter, Pocahontas. Powhatan was the leader of a powerful confederacy of Algonquian-speaking tribes numbering some 9,000 people. Along with Rolfe and Pocahontas, Powhatan attempted to maintain an uneasy peace between the Indians and the new settlers so that the two communities could coexist.

It was a difficult situation at best because the region had long been visited by slave traders from several countries. For nearly a century, Indians had been captured to become slaves elsewhere. Later, Africans were imported as slaves to work on the plantations, but in the early days greedy ship captains considered Indians a valuable cargo. When Powhatan died in 1618, he was succeeded by his brother, Opechancanough, who attacked Jamestown in 1622, killing settlers and destroying farms. The settlers retaliated by destroying the Indians' villages, crops, and canoes. This was typical of Indian-settler relations—vicious and brutal retaliation by both sides in a seemingly endless cycle.

Indians had been growing tobacco for centuries, but Europeans found the type of plant that they grew unpleasant. Rolfe, using the native plant, developed a milder strain that was more pleasing to European tastes. As tobacco became a major export, additional land was sought to increase production. More and more immigrants arrived in Virginia, putting more and more land under cultivation. The populations of game birds and animals on which the Indians depended were decimated, and the settlers' livestock destroyed the Indians' gardens. In 1644, an aged Opechancanough made a futile attack on the settlement. He was captured and killed, and the Tidewater Confederacy collapsed.

Indian Uprisings

The pattern of Indian-white conflict repeated itself even more violently in the Northeast. By 1630, there had been a large Puritan emigration into New England. A few years later, two English ship captains were killed by the Niantic, who were allies of the Pequot and Narraganset. Despite the victims' unsavory reputations, the Massachusetts Bay Colony authorized a mission to retaliate against the Pequot and the Block Island Nar-

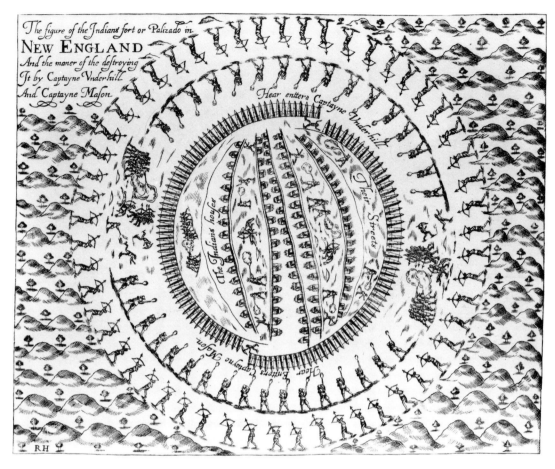

The figure of the Indians fort or Palizado in
NEW ENGLAND
And the maner of the destroying
It by Captayne Vnderhill
And Captayne Mason.

Hear enttera Captayne Vnderhill

Their Streets

The Indians howses

Hear Entters Captayne Mason

RH

raganset. The Pequot, who had not been a party to the killings, were angered by the military action and the imposed fines, and they sought revenge. The Pequot were all but exterminated in the resulting war. Survivors were enslaved and shipped to the West Indies or parceled out to farmers in Connecticut or Massachusetts. With the removal of the Pequot, more land was available for white settlement. Lieutenant Lion Gardiner, who led the mission, subsequently obtained large tracts of land, and Gardiners Island in Long Island Sound is still in the hands of his descendants.

Early Plymouth settlers were given aid by Massasoit, an important sachem of the Wampanoag. Generally, peaceful relations ensued for 40 years, until his death

A 1638 drawing shows the deployment of forces at the major battle of the Pequot War. A militia commissioned by the Massachusetts Bay Company attacked a stockaded Pequot village in Connecticut in reprisal for the death of two British traders. More than 600 Pequots died in this encounter, and in the next year virtually all the members of the tribe were killed or captured and sold into slavery.

in 1662. However, over the decades, the number of Europeans from Maine to Connecticut had increased, and they had secured more and more acreage for their farms. The Protestants who settled New England were noted for their zealous concern for righteousness and their lack of tolerance for the ways of others. They believed that Indians should be subject to their laws and moral code. Indians came to realize that their lifestyle was being destroyed, and sensing their loss, they finally resisted the advance of white settlements.

Metacomet (also called Philip), Massasoit's son and successor, formed a confederacy of several tribes—Narraganset, Nipmuck, Abenaki, and some Mohawk. Beginning in 1675, he led raids on the settlers that, in turn, were avenged by equally violent assaults by the settlers. For a time, it appeared that Metacomet's forces would be victorious over the colonists, but hunger resulting from the loss of food supplies contributed to their eventual defeat one year later. Metacomet's betrayal by one of his warriors led to his capture, and he was brutally killed in 1676. King Philip's War, as it came to be called, devastated the Narraganset and other tribes as entire Indian villages were massacred. Those who survived moved to the west and north, and settlers took over their lands, expanding farther into Indian territories.

In 1610, there were only a few hundred colonists on the east coast. By 1750, the population had increased to more than 1 million, and 2 million settlers lived along the narrow Atlantic corridor of the 13 colonies in 1770. This immense growth had been actively encouraged by British merchants who formed companies to develop colonies in North America. The London Company was one of the first to apply for and receive a charter and land grant from the British crown. In addition, land promoters could make large profits by inducing people from many countries to immigrate. Some schemes were legitimate; others were not. Some companies even used brochures that included extravagant descriptions of the world that awaited the settlers.

France and England Clash

Throughout the 17th and 18th centuries, the increasing entanglement of Great Britain and France in European politics involved the peoples of both the Old World and New World. The wars between the two European powers affected their affairs in North America, which, in turn, had a significant impact on Native Americans. At various times between 1689 and 1763, the North American continent became a battlefield on which European disagreements were vigorously contested, and Indians such as the Iroquois were at times either unwitting pawns or willing allies of the Europeans.

Warfare was conducted in a series of raids and counterraids, rather than battles. Even before King William's War had officially begun in Europe, tensions had heightened in North America as pro-French or pro-English Indians attacked each other. During that war, the Iroquois agreed to ratify a treaty with the French and other Indian groups. An important provision of the agreement was that the Iroquois would remain neutral in the conflict between France and England.

Queen Anne's War was a particularly brutal event in North America. British troops were insufficient in number, which left settlements vulnerable to raids by French forces and their Indian allies. Various Indian tribes also used the period to their advantage, such as dealing with merchants not legally empowered to trade with them. Some also found that it was profitable to attack other tribes. When England prevailed in Queen Anne's War, it obtained certain territorial and commercial advantages. Under the Treaty of Utrecht (1713), France ceded Nova Scotia, Newfoundland, and portions of the Hudson Bay region to the English. The war's end also opened free trade for the Indians, who could then exchange their furs with either France or England. After the war, the French moved swiftly to restore the lucrative fur trade, and the English began to enlarge their colonies along the Atlantic coast.

The French and Indian War

The French and Indian War began in 1754 with a quarrel over land—especially over who would possess the upper Ohio Valley. The war, which pitted white settlers and troops in British colonies and their Indian allies against the French and their Indian allies, began with French victories at Fort Necessity (1754) and Fort Duquesne (1755). By 1756, the conflict had escalated into a major worldwide war known in Europe as the Seven Years' War. England turned the tide of the war by sending large amounts of supplies and experienced troops to the colonies. France was defeated in North America in the fall of 1760. The Seven Years' War continued in Europe until 1763, when the war-weary nations negotiated the Treaty of Paris. The treaty gave England all of North America east of the Mississippi River, including Canada and Florida. France was allowed to keep New Orleans. France's Indian allies, who had been a lethal force in the outlying colonial settlements both in the North and in the South, were suddenly abandoned by the French and, in effect, handed over to their enemies.

The end of the French and Indian War did not mark the end of Indian hostilities. Pontiac, an Ottawa leader, established a formidable force by rallying other tribes—including the Huron, Delaware, and Shawnee—to continue the war against the British. Pontiac fought brilliantly, attacking British settlers in the spring of 1763 to remove them from Indian lands. His forces overran all the British posts except Fort Pitt and Fort Detroit. His surprise attack on Detroit was betrayed by an informer, and he was forced to lay siege to it.

Had Pontiac been able to maintain unity, the history of that region might have been different. Europeans had practiced long-term, sustained military campaigns for centuries. In contrast, Indian groups were accustomed to fighting intermittently. Instead of following up victories by pursuing total conquest, they returned to their villages to carry on the everyday business of living. Alignments tended not to last, and Pontiac's war was over by 1764 after his allies broke away. In 1766, he negotiated a peace treaty with Sir William Johnson, the British superintendent of Indian affairs (1756–74). Johnson was a potent force for friendly relations between Indians and whites.

As an inducement for peace between settlers and Indians in the fall of 1763, King George prohibited most westward expansion beyond the Allegheny Mountains. This was not out of altruism for Indians. Britain simply wanted to control the entire fur trade, and peaceful relations with the Indians were essential to the enterprise. Land speculation was thereby denied promoters, and new settlers were prohibited from obtaining acreage. Many colonists believed that King George upheld the rights of Indians over their own, and despite the royal edict settlers began moving into the forbidden lands. Some local treaties were negotiated, which gave the actions a semblance of legality.

A wagon train crosses Indian lands on its westward journey. The territory controlled by Indians shrank as the United States expanded its domain across the continent. Indians suffered an enormous loss of land, the catastrophic repercussions of which are still felt today.

LOSING GROUND

As the 18th century progressed, talented individuals in Europe were no longer willing to accept the rigid social and economic stratification in their homelands, and thousands left the nations of their birth for the English colonies in the New World. These immigrants, although diverse, carried with them certain common elements. They believed in the Christian God and dressed, worked, and thought in only Anglo-European ways. Perhaps most important, they believed in private property and individual ownership.

The European immigrants encountered a totally different cultural milieu in North America, where they found equally religious people who were devoted to unfamiliar spiritual beliefs and who held different attitudes toward property. The Indians' orientation to the world was vastly unlike that of the white settlers, and the majority of the immigrants could not or would not understand or appreciate the differences. For example, settlers viewed land as something to be used and worked. Value and profit came from productive exploitation of land as a resource. To the Indian, land was much more than simply a garden plot for growing corn or tobacco. It was a gift from the Creator. Above all, there was a critical sacredness associated with land and with all other things of nature. The products of the land—domestic and wild—sustained life.

The manner in which Indians and whites viewed the buffalo provides a clear example of their differing conceptions of the world and role of humans in the environment. The settler perceived the buffalo as a nuisance that knocked down fences, which were important to the pioneers both physically and psychologically. Fences enclosed the land that the settlers had claimed as their own. To the white hunter, the buffalo was an animal whose hide could be sold for use in the manufacture of shoes and belts. And occasionally its meat might be eaten. In contrast, Indians considered the buffalo as more than a source of food and other useful products. They perceived a spiritual relationship between themselves and the beast. For example, the buffalo was a symbol of healing and fertility for the Cheyenne, and among the Pawnee buffalo hunting was under the control of spiritual leaders and the success of the hunt was directly related to following the proper rituals. The wanton slaughter of the buffalo—such as shooting them from railroad car windows just for sport—was incomprehensible to Indians. As settlers pushed west, Indians saw their hunting territories increasingly constricted by fences. Both their and the buffalo's freedom were vanishing.

Before the American Revolution, several tribes had engaged in disputes over land. The Iroquois, for example, had yielded their claim to certain lands south of the Ohio and Susquehanna rivers in a treaty negotiated by Sir William Johnson in 1768. Johnson believed the treaty would safeguard the remaining Indian lands. As white settlers moved into the region, they committed serious atrocities against the Indians, who responded in kind. These raids and counterraids escalated into Lord Dunmore's War. Shawnee, Delaware, Mingo, Wyandot, Seneca, and Cayuga all became involved. The tribes were defeated in 1774 but continued to harbor anger against white settlers.

The American Revolution

In the years following the Seven Years' War, England became the world's major power. Spain controlled more territory, but England had greater wealth and embarked on vast and unprecedented commercial enterprises and technological developments that created the British Empire. In the face of this monumental endeavor, the American Revolution was an audacious act. The shots fired at Concord and Lexington in 1775 were a challenge to a supremely powerful monarch and the nation that he ruled.

At the beginning of the Revolution, Indian tribes were officially encouraged to remain neutral by the English and the Americans, but both the Loyalists and the revolutionaries solicited their aid. Most Indian groups joined the side of the English because their disputes were primarily with white settlers, not the English king. The Iroquois' location was a strategic one, and they were urged by their white friends to side with them. Many Seneca, Cayuga, Onondaga, and Mohawk fought in support of the British. The Oneida and some Tuscarora went with the Americans. The great confederacy of the Iroquois was split apart as its members battled one another.

Joseph Brant (Thayendanegea), a Mohawk chief, became one of the most notable Indians in the revolutionary war. As a youth he had fought in the French and Indian War under Sir William Johnson, and he attended Moor's Charity School for Indians in Connecticut, where he converted to Christianity. He also served as secretary to Sir Guy Johnson (nephew and son-in-law

Mohawk chief Thayendanegea, known as Joseph Brant, served as a captain in the English army during the Revolution. After the war, the English commander of Canada rewarded Brant for his services with a pension and land in Ontario. Other Iroquois, particularly the Mohawk, followed him to Canada. Brant became an active Anglican missionary until his death in 1807.

of Sir William) when Sir Guy became superintendent of Indian affairs in the north. Brant was commissioned as a captain in the English army in 1774. Seneca chiefs Cornplanter (Kaiiwontwakon) and Red Jacket (Sago-yewatha) also served as officers during the war.

In August of 1777, a fierce battle was fought at Oriskany, New York, near Fort Stanwix. The American general Nicholas Herkimer, in command of white and Oneida forces, was severely beaten by British troops. Several Seneca chiefs and a number of warriors were among the casualties. Loyalist Indians were angered at the Oneida's participation on the side of the colonists and burned one of their villages in retaliation. An Oneida force, in turn, burned some Mohawk dwellings. Later in the fall, English general John Burgoyne was defeated by General Horatio Gates with a force of Americans, Oneida, and Tuscarora. Without the Indian participation, the battle would have been lost.

During the Revolution, parts of New York and Pennsylvania were devastated by English-Indian raids, some under the leadership of Brant. The American major general John Sullivan was finally able to fight back in 1779 with sufficient force to take the war to previously untouched Iroquois villages. Several brigades destroyed the Indian crops and food supply, thereby leaving groups loyal to the English destitute during the long cold winter. The Oneida and Tuscarora villages felt their fellow Iroquois' wrath in retaliatory raids. In the southern colonies, prominent Britishers sought to enlist local tribes to fight on their side. Some Cherokee villages were subsequently devastated by the revolutionaries. The Creek and Choctaw fought bravely throughout the war on the side of the English, but the surrender at Yorktown, Virginia, placed them at the mercy of their American enemies. The Revolution left a legacy of animosity among both Indians and white settlers.

Renewed Hostilities

The Treaty of Paris (1783) did not address the question of the Indian tribes and the lands that they occupied. England ceded its former 13 colonies to the Americans and made no proper provision, such as an Indian territory, for its faithful allies. Even the Spanish, who had sided with the Americans, believed some arrangement should be made for them. The American position was tersely stated by John Jay: "We claim the right of preemption." In other words, the United States declared that it now controlled the lands ceded by England.

The Treaty of Paris, which created a sizable country for the United States, was intended to bring peace. In reality, it inaugurated the beginning of a new hostility between England and the United States—an economic war. From 1783 to 1812, England attempted to force the new American nation to its knees by using tariffs and trade regulations as weapons. However, war in Europe kept the English forces from attempting an invasion of the new nation and gave the neutral United States a great opportunity to participate in commerce abroad.

Indians were angered at their nonrecognition in the Paris peace treaty, and some continued to defend their lands and way of life. A new coalition developed, primarily among the Shawnee, Delaware, Wyandot, Ottawa, Potawatomi, Chippewa, and Miami. This new alignment protested confiscation of their areas by the United States and, among other things, asserted that the Ohio River was to be the boundary between whites and Indians.

In 1791, President George Washington recommended an Indian policy to Congress that he believed allowed for a humane coexistence of Native Americans and the new Americans. However eloquently stated, his philosophy of coexistence did not tolerate differences. Essentially, Indians were to change their ways and become like whites. Along with imparting to them all the blessings of Western civilized life, Washington guaranteed the Indians their lands. His grand design proved unsuccessful, particularly his assurance that Indian lands would be secure.

General Anthony Wayne's victory at the Battle of Fallen Timbers in 1795 brought a temporary peace to the Great Lakes area. The treaty signed in Greenville, Ohio, made important concessions to the Indians, including assuring their rights to the lands that they occupied. But with a degree of peace in the Northwest, more settlers came into the region. Once again a treaty was broken.

The Treaty of San Lorenzo (1795) with Spain gave Americans the right to travel on the Mississippi River. In 1803, the United States obtained the vast Louisiana Territory from France for $15 million, nearly doubling the size of the country. Exploration of the region by Merriwether Lewis and William Clark began in 1804 and created great public interest. In a few years, those Indian lands would also have whites arriving in wagons with their few possessions. Settlers from the East and newly arrived immigrants from Europe believed that any region under the U.S. flag was available to them. It was a common white attitude that "Indians did not use the land."

By the end of the 18th century, land in New England and in parts of the South was already worn thin by overplanting, and fields under intensive cultivation for tobacco had become exhausted. With the development of the cotton gin in 1793, cotton became a profitable crop, establishing a plantation economy requiring vast acreage that only existed to the west. Freed from the restraints placed on expansion by King George, former colonists were able to move west at will. The United States grew with the arrival of new immigrants, and the demand for more territory escalated. The first U.S. census in 1790 counted nearly 4 million people. By 1800, the population had grown to more than 5 million, and by the end of the 19th century it would swell to nearly 76 million.

Resisting the Influx of Whites

As the governor of the Indiana Territory (1800–1812), William Henry Harrison succeeded in obtaining more than 3 million acres of land for white settlement by dealing with corrupt chiefs who did not represent their tribes. Harrison's efforts were challenged by Tecumseh, one of the greatest Indian leaders. Tecumseh, a Shawnee chief, and his brother Tenskwatawa, a medicine man, succeeded in pulling together a coalition of tribes in an attempt to stop Harrison's acquisitions of Indian land. Tecumseh traveled widely urging other tribes to withstand white encroachment. In November 1811, Harrison launched an attack on Prophetstown, Tecumseh's settlement on the banks of the Tippecanoe River, during the chief's absence. The destruction of the village provoked the tribes to seek revenge with arms supplied by the English.

The War of 1812, fought between the United States and England, erupted a few months later. The U.S. Army often encountered Indians fighting for England. But those warriors were not fighting someone else's war; it was a war for their tribal sovereignty. The war

During the Battle of the Thames in the War of 1812, U.S. troops under the command of Richard M. Johnson battle Indian forces. Shawnee chief Tecumseh (foreground), who had attempted to form a confederacy among many Indian tribes to resist white encroachment, died during the battle while fighting on the side of the English.

raged on with victories and defeats on both sides. The English marched into the nation's capital in Washington and burned the Capitol and the White House. Americans assumed that Canada would be an easy conquest, but the English, Canadian, and Indian forces held firm until Oliver Hazard Perry's naval victory on Lake Erie in 1813. In October of that year, Harrison's troops won the decisive Battle of the Thames (Canada) in which Tecumseh and other chiefs were slain.

A few months later, General Andrew Jackson led a force of 3,500 Tennessee militiamen against the Red Stick faction of the Creek nation, which had killed 400 settlers in a raid on Fort Mims in present-day Alabama. In March 1814, Jackson's troops soundly defeated the Creek at their stronghold in Horseshoe Bend. By removing the Creek from their lands, Jackson opened the Mississippi Valley for future white settlement, and his victory over the Creek, coupled with Harrison's success over Tecumseh, broke the spirit of the Indian uprisings east of the Mississippi.

Andrew Jackson's Legacy

The War of 1812 concluded with the signing of the Treaty of Ghent on December 24, 1814. Not knowing the war was over, both sides kept fighting, and Andrew Jackson's army won the Battle of New Orleans, considered the greatest U.S. victory of the war. Jackson emerged from the War of 1812 as a popular hero, and President James Monroe appointed him commander of the U.S. Army's Southern District. His main task was to defend Georgia from Indians who raided from Florida (then a Spanish possession). It was inevitable that Jackson, a believer in territorial expansion, would challenge Spanish rule. He invaded Florida, and after minimal diplomatic exchanges, Spain ceded the territory to the United States in 1819.

Jackson was a product of frontier existence—its best and its worst. He had experienced the brutal reprisals between Indians and white settlers, a condition that had been characteristic from the time of the first colonies. Jackson became president of the United States in 1829 and carried his old animosities with him into the White House. During his eight years in office, Jackson directly influenced policies that would lead to the widespread loss of Indian land and massive Indian displacement.

The Creek still held vast tracts of fertile land under a treaty with the federal government. When Georgia appropriated their holdings, the Creek appealed the state's confiscation before the Supreme Court. When the Court ruled against Georgia, Jackson made no attempt to enforce its ruling, thereby allowing the state to retain the lands. The president's actions, allowing a state to overrule national authority, sent a clear message to the white population: Indian land could be trespassed with impunity.

Perhaps Jackson's most notorious action was to convince Congress to pass the Indian Removal Act (1830), which required Indians living in the East and Southeast to give up their land in exchange for land in unsettled territories west of the Mississippi. Some legislators voted for the bill because they believed that the reservation solution was the only alternative to ensure the Indians' survival. Once the bill was enacted, it engendered irreparable harm. Between 1830 and 1840, more than 50,000 Indians were forced to leave their homes and move to Indian Territory (present-day Oklahoma). The Cherokee, Creek, Chickasaw, Seminole, and Choctaw were among the tribes herded west by the federal government. Members of the Cherokee tribe left in mid-winter on what became known as the Trail of Tears. During the 800-mile exodus, at least 4,000 Cherokees died from exposure and starvation.

Some Indians resisted the U.S. government's removal policy. In 1832, Black Hawk, a chief of the Illinois Sauk who had fought with the British in the War of 1812, led a portion of the Sauk and Fox tribes in armed

The Trail of Tears, *an 1840 painting by Robert Lindneux, shows the anguish of the Cherokee during their forced migration from their lands in the Southeast. On the journey west to present-day Oklahoma, between one-fourth and one-half of the Cherokee died of exhaustion, exposure, or disease.*

revolt against federal troops assigned to oversee the removal. Black Hawk's forces conducted raids against white settlements and eluded the U.S. Army for several months before finally being overcome.

Led by Chief Osceola, some Seminole also resisted relocation. Fighting from bases in the Florida everglades, Osceola's forces were victorious, and in 1837 he agreed to meet under a flag of truce proposed by the Americans. The parley was a hoax, and Osceola was seized and imprisoned in South Carolina, where he died of malaria a few months later. Other Seminole fought on until 1842. Although most Seminole then moved to Indian Territory, some refused to surrender and survived by living in the swamps of the everglades. Portions of a few other Indian tribes, including part of the eastern Cherokee, managed to avoid removal. But by the mid-1840s, a large number of tribes that once inhabited the eastern United States had been forced to move to areas west of the Mississippi.

White pioneers gathered speed in their westward expansion. By 1825, some 75 steamboats were navigating the Mississippi, and the Erie Canal opened that same year, creating an all-water route into the heartland of the continent. A person could travel from Massachusetts to Michigan for little more than $10. By 1836, Detroit had a population of 10,000, a library, a museum, a public garden, and some streetlights, and Chicago had become a center of transportation and industry.

During the tenure of President James K. Polk (1845–49), the United States obtained even more land for settlement. In 1846, war was declared between Mexico and the United States. With the fall of Mexico City in 1847, the Mexican war was over. In accordance with the Treaty of Guadalupe Hidalgo (1848), Mexico relinquished two-fifths of its territory to the United States. The Rio Grande was accepted as the southern boundary of Texas, and California and New Mexico became U.S. territories. The United States paid Mexico $15 million and forgave all of Mexico's debts.

The discovery of gold in California in 1848 lured prospectors and others to California. California became a state in 1850, and Oregon followed in 1859. Gold and silver were soon discovered in western Nevada, prompting another influx of newcomers. The United States also obtained additional land in the northwest by treaty with England. By 1860, the nation's population was more than 23 million. Native Americans from the Atlantic to the Pacific and from Canada to Mexico were engulfed by settlers.

Chief Osceola led the Seminole resistance to the U.S. government's removal policy from 1835 until his death in an army prison in 1838.

The Last Battles

Classic Plains culture reached its peak with the coming of the horse but soon ended with the overwhelming advance of settlers. Fur trappers from Canada and the East moved into their region and beyond. Initially, the few white settlers had limited impact, but the diseases that they brought devastated populations. For example, the Mandan and Hidatsa tribes of North Dakota lived in densely populated earth-lodge villages at the time of European contact. In the smallpox epidemic of 1837–38, seven-eighths of the Mandan and half of the Hidatsa perished.

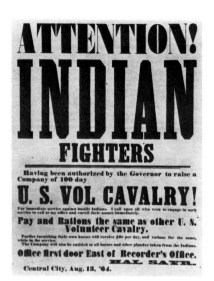

ATTENTION!
INDIAN
FIGHTERS

Having been authorized by the Governor to raise a
Company of 100 day

U. S. VOL CAVALRY!

For immediate service against hostile Indians. I call upon all who wish to engage in such
service to call at my office and enroll their names immediately.

Pay and Rations the same as other U. S.
Volunteer Cavalry.

Parties furnishing their own horses will receive 40c per day, and rations for the same,
while in the service.
The Company will also be entitled to all horses and other plunder taken from the Indians.

Office first door East of Recorder's Office.
HAL SAYR.

Central City, Aug. 13, '64.

An advertisement appearing in a Colorado newspaper in 1864 seeks Indian fighters. The U.S. Cavalry needed short-term volunteers to replace troops engaged in the Civil War.

As white hunters slaughtered the buffalo in increasing numbers, they reduced the Indian food supply, a fact that did not go unnoticed by the U.S. Army. General Philip H. Sheridan believed that buffalo hunters deserved the nation's thanks because it would be easier for the army to end Indian resistance on the Plains with the buffalo gone. Indians saw the Santa Fe and Oregon trails cut into the earth by countless wagons bringing settlers into their lands. In 1869, the Union Pacific and the Central Pacific railroads joined at Promontory, Utah, and soon other rails crisscrossed the Plains.

In an effort to protect pioneers, the federal government attempted to have Indians guarantee them safe passage and sought to restrict Indian hunting to only certain regions. In return, the government proposed to offer trade goods. Several treaties were formulated but proved fruitless. The discovery of precious metals brought still more whites onto Indian lands in search of fortune. Beginning in the 1850s, ambushes and bloody massacres regularly took the lives of Indians, settlers, and soldiers. For the next 30 years the Plains were aflame with fighting. Some Indians sought solace in messianic movements, such as the Ghost Dance religion, that were intended to restore Indian lifeways.

Indians fought fiercely to preserve their lands and their way of life. In the Far West, Indians under leaders such as Chief Joseph of the Nez Percé resisted the incursions of whites and forced relocation to reservations. Once again the superior weaponry of the whites overcame the resistance of the Indians. Whenever the Indians triumphed, more U.S. troops appeared to fight anew.

The Civil War not only divided white Americans but also disrupted Indian tribes and alliances. In the 1860s, regular Union troops were pulled from the West to fight the Confederates, with whom some tribes were allied. Short-term local volunteers were pressed into service to fight western Indians. For example, advertisements in 1864 called for Colorado volunteers for the

U.S. Cavalry. Along with regular pay and rations, the prospective recruits were further enticed by "all horses and other plunder taken from the Indians."

It was the beginning of the end in 1876 when a vastly superior force of Sioux warriors led by Sitting Bull and Crazy Horse outmaneuvered and routed the cavalry troops of Lieutenant Colonel George Armstrong Custer at the Battle of Little Bighorn. It was the Indians' last military victory. Shortly afterward, resisting bands were either systematically killed or forced to surrender and placed on reservations. Crazy Horse was stabbed in the back while resisting imprisonment. Sitting Bull and his followers escaped to Canada after Little Bighorn, but Sitting Bull surrendered in 1881. Nine years later he was killed by reservation police while resisting arrest on a charge of rebellion. A short time later, the mindless slaughter of the Sioux by vengeful U.S. troops at a camp called Wounded Knee ended armed Indian resistance.

A detail from Sioux warrior Red Horse's 1881 pictograph depicts the Battle of Little Bighorn in present-day Montana. Sioux forces under the command of Sitting Bull and Crazy Horse killed all 200 men in a detachment of the Seventh Cavalry led by George Armstrong Custer. Custer's Last Stand, a tremendous victory for Indians, rallied whites to escalate the conquest of hostile Indian groups.

Yakima chiefs Frank Seelatse (left) and Jimmy Noah Saluskin pose in front of the Capitol while in Washington, D.C., to confer with Congress on land rights in the early 20th century.

REFORM, RECOVERY, AND REVITALIZATION

The history of Indian-white relations can be viewed as the story of land and its use and control. The displacement of Indians from their lands by European colonists and the generations that succeeded them in westward expansion and settlement continued for more than 400 years. When the Europeans arrived in the late 15th century, Indians held nearly 2 billion acres in the present-day United States. Indian lands now total only about 96 million acres. Policies to remove Indians from their land and to sequester them on reservations developed early on. The first federal Indian reservation was established in 1786. Reservations may have been well intentioned, but the concept was ultimately unsuccessful. Some reservation land was good, but much of it was either infertile or arid. The resources of reservations were typically inadequate for self-sufficiency.

After the American Revolution, Congress placed Indian affairs under the jurisdiction of the War Department. On his own initiative, Secretary of War John C. Calhoun took the unorthodox step of establishing the Indian Department as an independent branch in 1824 and renaming it the Bureau of Indian Affairs (BIA). Congress, which usually creates federal agencies by enacting legislation, officially recognized the bureau's independent status in 1834.

The BIA was transferred to the newly created Department of the Interior in 1849. As Indians began to move onto reservations in the 1850s and 1860s, the bureau became responsible for overseeing the activities of the reservations. On each reservation, the BIA established an agency consisting of an office building, a school, a dormitory, barns, stables, storehouses, and housing for BIA employees. Some agents (BIA officials who lived among Indian tribes and administered policies at the local level) were honest in their dealings with Indians, but others were corrupt. At times, unscrupulous agents improperly sold food rations to non-Indians or withheld it as punishment for some infraction. The reservation system was a failure for most Indians. Game, water, and good farmland were inadequate in such restricted territory. People could not support themselves and grew dependent upon government food allotments. Idleness and loss of spirit followed. The placement of Indians on reservations failed to eliminate friction with whites and made the reservations seem more like penal institutions than anything else.

Reservations remain a mixed blessing today. Fragmented by non-Indian landholdings, political infighting, and disagreements over bingo games and other forms of gambling, many reservations are in turmoil. In addition, widespread uncertainties about law enforcement and sovereignty create distress among many reservation residents. Indians speak of themselves as comprising nations—and once they did. But today theirs is a limited sovereignty, subject to the will of the federal government.

In 1887, Congress passed the General Allotment Act (also known as the Dawes Severalty Act), which led to Indians losing nearly two-thirds of their reservation lands. Under this act, a number of reservations were subdivided into tracts of 40, 80, and 160 acres that were alloted to individual Indians as private holdings. The deed to the land was to be held by the federal government for 25 years or longer if deemed necessary, then given to the individual along with citizenship. The remaining unallotted lands were declared surplus and made available to non-Indians. Because many Indians were not interested in or skilled at agriculture or cattle raising and because some allotted land was poor or too small to produce an adequate income, many allotments were sold cheaply. By 1933, more than 90 million acres had been lost by Indians.

This farm on the Yankton Sioux reservation in South Dakota was created by the General Allotment Act of 1887. Under this act, some reservations were subdivided into smaller tracts that were then given to individual Indians as private holdings. Land that was not allotted was declared surplus and sold to non-Indians.

Trends Since 1900

In the early years of the 20th century, there was a growing awareness that the government's Indian policy was flawed. The assimilation of Indians into the larger society that had so long been advocated was not working. At the same time, dissatisfaction with the BIA and its management of Indian programs increased. In 1923, President Warren Harding appointed a national advisory group of leading citizens to recommend improvements in the administration of Indian affairs. The committee urged that Indians receive better education and health care; that the court of claims be opened to Indian tribes; and that solutions be found to certain land questions, particularly among the Pueblo. Calvin Coolidge, who succeeded Harding, acted quickly on these recommendations. In 1924, Congress passed the Indian Citizenship Act, enabling Indians to vote. That same year, Congress enacted legislation concerning Pueblo lands and passed a bill that approved the payment of tuition for Indian children who wished to attend public schools.

Two important studies with far-reaching implications were also undertaken in the late 1920s. One analyzed the BIA, and the other, called *The Problem of Indian Administration* (also known as the Meriam Report), stressed the poverty of Indians and their lack of inclusion in the dominant society. The report particularly criticized the allotment policy of the federal government, pointing to the substantial loss of land by Indians. Along with other studies conducted in the late 1920s and early 1930s, these reports and the growing disenchantment with federal Indian policies and programs helped prepare the way for the passage of the Indian Reorganization Act.

The Indian Reorganization Act

The Indian Reorganization Act of 1934 marked a dramatic turning point in federal Indian policy. The act ended the process of allotment of reservations lands, banned the unregulated sale of Indian lands, and authorized funds to purchase new lands for tribes. The ac also directed the secretary of the interior to draft

In April 1938, Commissioner of Indian Affairs John Collier (center) meets two representatives of the Crow tribe who were in Washington, D.C., to confer with Collier about tribal matters. During Collier's administration (1933–45), the federal government's Indian policy sought to preserve the tribal groups of Indians and to assure full Indian democracy.

regulations governing rangeland grazing and logging and initiated a system of federal loans for tribal economic development. But the most important part of the act asserted the right of Indians to govern themselves and enabled tribes to organize as corporations for the management of tribal business enterprises. Under the inspired leadership of John Collier, the newly appointed commissioner of Indian affairs, Indians took a critical step forward toward self-government. Not all Indians, however, perceived that the legislation was beneficial. The bill called for ratification by Indian tribes, allowing them to choose whether or not the act would apply to them. In the end, 181 tribes with a population of 129,750 Indians voted to accept the act, and 77 tribes with a population of 86,365 rejected it.

Pima children and adults attend class at a reservation school in the early 20th century. Many schools were built on reservations to overcome the disadvantages of government-sponsored, off-reservation boarding schools. Boarding schools such as the Carlisle School in Pennsylvania removed young Indians from their home environments to hasten their acculturation to white society and to eradicate their fluency in Indian languages.

During the mid-1930s, tribes slowly began the process of adopting constitutions and corporate charters that were designed to strengthen tribal governments. On the economic side, tribes were eligible to receive credit for agricultural and business projects through a revolving-loan fund. A great number of Indian schools were built on reservations to overcome the disadvantages of being away from home at boarding schools.

World War II dominated global affairs for many years, beginning in the late 1930s. Everything else, including Indian affairs, became subordinate. Because government expenditures were used largely to support the war effort, domestic programs suffered cutbacks. Both BIA officials and young men from the reservations entered military service, and other Indians sought employment in war-related industries away from the reservations. Tribal enterprises diminished in strength or were suspended for lack of participants. After the war, many Indians stayed in the cities where they had found employment, and many returning servicemen found a return to reservation life unacceptable.

The Indian Claims Commission

In 1946, Congress passed the Indian Claims Commission Act, allowing tribes to file their legal claims against the U.S. government. The long-standing desire by Indians for redress of perceived wrongs, particularly the seizure of their lands without proper compensation, provided one of the main reasons for the formation of the commission. Some supporters of the act pointed out that by 1940 Indians possessed slightly more than two percent of the land in the United States. No payment was ever made for tens of millions of acres that they had lost, and much additional acreage was ceded in the course of treaty negotiations for very little monetary or other compensation.

On the face of it, the passage of the Indian Claims Commission Act appeared to have been advantageous to Indians, but there was another motive. The claims commission was designed in part to enable the federal government to withdraw services from the tribes. Some legislators believed that tribes would become self-sufficient when they received awards. The act provided for monetary awards rather than land, and the expensive legal process was a hardship for many claimants. Even when awards were made, they were exceptionally conservative because land was valued at the time it was taken rather than at current market value. Moreover, in most cases the interest that would have accrued if the land would have been purchased at the original price was not taken into account. On the average, compensation was paid at less than a dollar an acre. The government's legal expenses and offsets (the value of goods and services that the government provided to the claimants after the claim arose) were deducted from the award in some cases. In the few cases where awards were made, Indians used the money to purchase land. More than 100 claims made between 1946 and 1951 have yet to be decided and were transferred to the court of claims when the commission was abolished in 1978.

Termination

The predominant attitude in Congress at the close of World War II was to discourage federal responsibility in

Two Navajo marines operate a portable radio during the United States's Pacific campaign in World War II. The U.S. Marine Corps adopted Navajo as a voice code because only an estimated 28 non-Navajos understood the language. More than 400 Navajos served as code talkers in Marine signal units during the war, enabling classified information to be transmitted rapidly.

The home of an elderly Menominee couple shows the effect of poverty three years after the federal government terminated its relationship with the Menominee tribe in 1961. The health and welfare of many Indians, including the Menominee, declined sharply after their tribes were terminated. Congress reinstated the Menominee to federal trust status in 1973.

Indian affairs. By 1950, many politicians favored the termination of all federal services to Indians, which they felt the individual states should provide. In 1953, Congress declared that the long-standing special relationship between Indians and the federal government was to end and that the tax-exempt status of Indian lands would no longer exist.

During the termination era (1954–66), Congress severed the federal relationship with more than 100 tribes, most of which were small groups located in California and Oregon. Two large tribes—the Menominee of Wisconsin and the Klamath of Oregon—were also terminated. Termination was a short-lived policy that did not work, but its effect on Indians was severe. Among the Menominee, for example, poverty, high infant mortality, illness, and housing and educational disadvantages ensued. By 1972, the BIA recommended that the Menominee tribe be returned to a trust relationship and services be resumed. Congress passed the necessary legislation the following year.

A Reversal in Government Policy

The 1960s was a pivotal decade for Indians in the United States. The Kennedy and Johnson administrations engineered a number of policy changes that benefited Indians. The Area Redevelopment Administration (now called the Economic Development Administration) was created within the Commerce Department in 1961. It financed the construction of community and cultural centers, tribal headquarters buildings, and tribal museums. In receiving money for federal projects, tribal governments were treated the same as non-Indian local governments. At long last, the operation of programs and the funds that supported them were placed in the hands of Indians.

As part of President Lyndon Johnson's War on Poverty, the Office of Economic Opportunity gave special attention to Indian poverty. It set an example for other federal agencies that also acknowledged tribes as sponsoring agencies for economic development, education, and other programs. At the same time, the civil rights legislation of the period provided for the employment of minorities, and Indians began to work for the federal government in far greater number, even for the BIA. Although Indians administered the federal programs, they did so along guidelines handed down to them from Washington. Tribal government became an extension of the federal government.

Indian Civil Rights and Activism

Throughout the 1960s, minority groups, including Indians, were active in protests and in the pursuit to secure civil rights, and activists took increasingly militant stands. In 1961, representatives of 67 tribes attended a conference in Chicago to attract attention to the historic role of Indians in the United States and their contemporary needs. The delegates adopted a relatively mild Declaration of Indian Purpose. The statement, however, did not meet the aspirations of some younger Indians, who decided to take new initiatives themselves. Later in 1961, this faction founded a new pan-Indian organization, the National Indian Youth Council (NIYC), as a means of instilling pride in Indians and pressing for their right to rule themselves. The NIYC urged reverence in respect to cultural traditions and adopted a previously absent activism. It also published a newspaper, participated in fishing rights demonstrations in the state of Washington, and offered counsel to tribes on important policy issues. The NIYC took part in the National Poor People's Campaign in 1968 and in the takeover of the BIA building in Washington, D.C., four years later.

In 1968, Indian activism turned more militant as the American Indian Movement (AIM) was founded. AIM began in Minneapolis as an urban Indian coalition, grew in strength, and received much public attention over the

Drummers beat out a rhythm for dancers at the American Indian Charter Convention held in Chicago in 1961. Representatives of 67 tribes attended the conference to discuss common problems and to attract attention to Indian issues. The delegates issued a Declaration of Indian Purpose, which called for increased Indian participation in the decision-making process of government programs that affected Indians.

In June 1973, two Indians stand guard outside the Sacred Heart Catholic Church during the American Indian Movement's (AIM) occupation of the site of the 1890 Wounded Knee Massacre. The activists seized Wounded Knee to demand reforms in the Sioux tribal government and a review of all Indian treaties. The occupation evolved into a 72-day standoff between armed activists and law enforcement authorities in which 2 Indians were killed and 1 police officer wounded.

next few years. AIM members participated in the Trail of Broken Treaties Caravan, a 1972 march on Washington, D.C., to present their demands for a change in the legal status of Indians to President Richard Nixon. The march culminated in the occupation of the BIA building.

AIM captured the attention of the world in 1973 when it seized Wounded Knee, a village on the Pine Ridge Sioux Reservation in South Dakota. In a tense confrontation with federal and local authorities, the Indians who occupied the town demanded a review of all Indian treaties and reforms in the Sioux tribal government. AIM's fortunes declined in subsequent years as it became involved in non-Indian human rights battles.

In 1969, a small group of Indian students from the University of California at Berkeley and San Francisco

State College seized control of Alcatraz Island in San Francisco Bay. The students, calling themselves Indians of All Tribes, occupied the abandoned federal prison on the island to press their demand that Indian lands illegally obtained by the federal government be returned. Although their effort fell short of their goal, the group succeeded in calling dramatic attention to the plight of Indians and in gaining the support of many Indians who joined the occupation.

Self-determination

In a special message to Congress in 1968, President Johnson announced a new policy of self-determination for Indians. He called for the end of termination and pledged to continue to help Indians relocate to communities where they could find employment. Much of Johnson's Indian policy was an outgrowth of 1960 campaign promises and programs begun in the Kennedy years, but the self-determination focus was Johnson's alone. He pressed for passage of the Indian Civil Rights Act of 1968, which advanced reforms in tribal government and tribal courts and underscored constitutional guarantees of religious freedom.

During the 1970s, President Nixon, outspokenly opposed to the philosophy of termination, supported self-determination, and his administration strove to be responsive to Indian demands for reform. In 1971, Congress passed the Alaska Native Claims Settlement Act, which provided for Indian ownership of 44 million acres of land and created a $1 billion trust fund for the use of more than 200 community-based Indian corporations. In addition, several terminated tribes were restored to trust status. Perhaps the most important legislation of this period to be passed by Congress was the Indian Self-Determination and Educational Assistance Act of 1975, under which funds for education were increased and the roles of tribal councils in the administration of federal programs were enlarged.

In November 1969, 9 of the 200 Indians who occupied the former prison island of Alcatraz stand under a sign that they had revised to reflect their position. The group seized the island, located in San Francisco Bay, to demand a meeting with the secretary of the interior to discuss ownership of the island, which had been declared surplus by the federal government. The island remained in Indian hands until mid-1971.

In 1986, demonstrators, objecting to the relocation of Navajo in northern Arizona, march outside the Bureau of Indian Affairs office in Phoenix. Indians have remained politically active during the end of the 20th century in order to secure the rights and benefits that they believe they deserve.

By contrast, the 1980s was a time of reduction of government commitments to Indians. Cutbacks in educational and other programs during the administration of Ronald Reagan led to the dismissal of some Indian claims, the deterioration of reservation programs, and greatly increased Indian unemployment. Nonetheless, in 1983 Reagan affirmed that termination was wrong and pledged his support for the Indian Self-Determination Act. In practice, his administration adhered to the philosophy of the termination era, insisting that there be a reduction in Indian dependence on federal revenues and a greater reliance upon private enterprise in the generation of investment capital.

During the 1980s, Congress and state legislatures passed measures calling for the repatriation of identifiable human remains to appropriate tribes or other groups who request them. The remains are usually reburied with proper religious observations. In other cases, questionable displays of skeletal remains in private, nonprofessional establishments have been halted. Museums with skeletal collections tend to recognize Indian sensibilities and attempt to cooperate. Increasingly, claims are also being made for the repatriation of cultural artifacts in museum collections that have real or purported religious importance. The determination of whether items have sacred or ceremonial value is difficult and controversial. Sympathetic as museum authorities may be to native views, they have trouble balancing repatriation requests with their responsibilities to maintain collections for research and education. Both Indians and museum people are seeking acceptable compromises.

A Century of Change

At the beginning of the 20th century, the Indian community was at its lowest point, both in numbers and in cultural vigor. But the remnant population of native people slowly began to recover, and the persistence of traditional ways has been remarkable. The achievements of this period have been extraordinary, although their evolution has come about at an excruciatingly slow pace. At the same time, enormous problems continue to exist. Most Indians, whether they live on reservations or in urban or rural communities off the reservations, are poverty-stricken. The 1980 census reported that 28 percent of Indians were living below the federal government's poverty threshold of $7,412 for a family of 4. And 45 percent of the nearly 340,000 Indians living on reservations were living below the poverty level, nearly 4 times higher than the national average of 12 percent.

Indians also have a high rate of unemployment, particularly on reservations where unemployment runs as high as 40 percent. Nearly half of the reservation population do not graduate from high school, which means that many do not have sufficient education to prepare them for a large number of skilled jobs. In general, their housing is substandard; alcoholism is chronic in many communities as both a reaction to and a further contribution to widespread malaise and despair. The incidence of suicide, particularly among the young, is high compared to the rest of society. Despite government-sponsored health programs, malnutrition and a high incidence of illness are found among reservation dwellers.

Oscar Howe's abstract painting Dance of the Heyoka *combines elements of modern art and traditional Indian art. Indians today are proud of their traditional ways, seeking to preserve their heritage while also adapting to the modern world.*

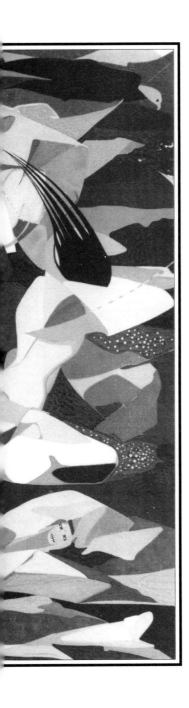

CONTEMPORARY INDIANS

At the end of the 15th century, the isolation of the Indian peoples of the Americas came to an end. The impact of European discovery ultimately spread to every corner of the hemisphere. Now, 500 years later—after the attrition caused by disease, conquest, and displacement; after missionizing, economic deprivation, and domination by the federal government; after suffering enormous losses of life, territory, and culture—Indians remain. Not only do they remain, but they are growing in numbers.

The 1980 census identified about 500 Indian tribes and bands of greatly varying sizes. Ninety percent of these had populations of fewer than 10,000. The 10 largest tribes were the Cherokee (232,080), Navajo (158,633), Sioux (78,608), Chippewa (73,602), Choctaw (50,220), Pueblo (42,552), Iroquois Confederacy (38,218), Apache (35,861), Lumbee (28,631), and Creek (28,278). Most Native Americans live west of the Mississippi

River, with the highest concentration of people living in California. In 1980, more than half of them lived in just five states—California, Oklahoma, Arizona, New Mexico, and North Carolina.

The 1980 census also revealed that 25 percent of the Indian population (340,000) were living on the 278 federal and state reservations, and another 9 percent (116,000) were living in historic areas of Oklahoma. Reservations of varying sizes exist in 35 states. The largest, the Navajo Reservation, encompasses nearly 16 million acres in Arizona, New Mexico, and Utah. The smallest, the Golden Hill Reservation (Paugusset Indians) in Connecticut, is only one-quarter acre.

Making Their Mark

From the earliest days of contact with whites, many outstanding Indians have achieved honor and distinction as warriors, statesmen, artists, scholars, and sports figures. Tecumseh, Osceola, Geronimo, Seattle, Chief Joseph, Ishi, Crazy Horse, Sitting Bull, Cochise, and Red Cloud are all great personalities from the past. There will never be another Jim Thorpe, Will Rogers, or Chief Dan George. Charles Curtis (Kaw) was the only Indian vice-president of the United States (1929–33). There are many more whose names, talents, and deeds have gone unremembered.

Many Indians today influence policy, change minds, create beauty, argue for what they believe in, represent their people, and keep their balance while walking with a foot in each of two cultures. For example, Dr. Clara Sue Kidwell (Choctaw/Chippewa) heads the Native Studies Program at the University of California at Berkeley. Archaeologist Edmund Ladd (Zuni), attorney Walter EchoHawk (Pawnee), and authors Louise Erdrich (Chippewa), Michael A. Dorris (Modoc), and Leslie Marmon Silko (Laguna) contribute their singular talents to the benefit of society.

Vine Deloria, Jr., a member of the Standing Rock Sioux tribe, has written more cogently about Indians than anyone else. Deloria was born on the Pine Ridge Indian Reservation in South Dakota in 1933. He received a bachelor's degree from Iowa State University and a master's degree in theology from Augustana College in Illinois. (Both his father and grandfather were Episcopal priests.) A former executive director of the National Congress of American Indians, Deloria taught for many years at the University of Arizona in Tucson, where he developed a graduate program in American Indian Policy Studies. In 1990, he joined the faculty at the University of Colorado in Boulder.

After earning a law degree from the University of Colorado in 1970, Deloria founded the Institute for the Development of American Indian Law. He is a frequent speaker and commentator on contemporary Indian affairs. Deloria's first book, *Custer Died for Your Sins* (1969), written for a young audience, addresses issues that many younger people may have been unaware of and deals with reasons why Indians may harbor negative feelings toward whites. In *God Is Red* (1973), he compares Indian tribal religions with Christianity, and in *The Metaphysics of Modern Existence* (1979) he offers a non-Western outline of philosophical views.

Another renowned Indian author, N. Scott Momaday, received a Pulitzer Prize in 1969 for his novel *House Made of Dawn*, which tells the tragic story of how the life of a Kiowa unravels as he attempts to adjust to an urban environment. Momaday received his bachelor's degree from the University of New Mexico and his master's and doctorate from Stanford University. He taught at the University of California at Berkeley and Stanford and is currently a professor of English at the University of Arizona in Tucson.

Indians have a rich legacy in the arts. Countless persons are today acknowledged for their creativity in various media. In the late 19th and early 20th centuries,

Indians make leather moccasins at a factory located on a reservation. Many Indians are employed in the crafts industry, producing a wide variety of beautiful and practical items.

a number of Native Americans practiced their traditional crafts. Often their only customers were tourists. Despite their lack of recognition, those men and women served as teachers and provided models for younger tribal members. Today commercial galleries and museums seek the work of numerous native painters, potters, sculptors, weavers, and silversmiths. Some have found inspiration in their traditional heritage; others combine the old with the modern.

Any listing of contemporary artisans would be incomplete, but among them are Arthur D. Amiotte (Sioux), Grey Cohoe (Navajo), Grace Medicine Flower (Santa Clara Pueblo), R. C. Gorman (Navajo), Charles Loloma (Hopi), Oscar Howe (Yankton Sioux), Phyllis Fife (Creek), Al Momaday (Kiowa), Fritz Scholder (Luiseño Mission). A number of today's prominent artists received training or impetus from Lloyd Kiva New (Cherokee), the longtime director of the Institute of American Indian Arts and chairman of the Indian Arts and Crafts Board of the U.S. Department of the Interior.

María Martínez (Pueblo) was a renowned Native American potter whose work has been exhibited in major museums throughout the world. She was known for her sophisticated, lustrous black-on-black ware that is perfectly shaped and balanced without the use of a potter's wheel. In the early 1900s, Martínez and her husband, Julian, revived ancient Indian pottery-making methods that were suggested by shards found in an excavation of funeral mounds. After Julian's death in 1943, Martínez continued to work with her children and other villagers, and the craft business that they built revitalized the San Ildefonso Pueblo in New Mexico. Martínez died in 1980 at the age of 98.

In the world of dance, sisters Maria and Marjorie Tallchief (Osage) both became noted ballet dancers. In 1946, Maria, already an accomplished dancer, married dancer-choreographer George Ballanchine, and in the following year she joined his company, which became the New York City Ballet in 1948. She later joined the

American Ballet Theatre. Marjorie was one of the principal dancers of the Grand Ballet de Monte Carlo in Europe.

Many Indians have worked tirelessly to protect resources and preserve tribal culture. For example, social worker and teacher Ada Deer served as the chairperson of the Menominee Restoration Committee and as a lobbyist for the National Committee to Save Menominee People and Forest. She led a faction of the tribe that lobbied for repeal of termination. In 1973, Congress reversed itself, and the Menominee's relationship with the federal government was resumed. Patricia Zell (Navajo) holds a law degree and a Ph.D. in clinical psychology and is a principal aide to the chairman

Master potter María Martínez molds a bowl while her husband Julian paints a finished piece. Martínez's distinctive black-on-black work revived ancient Indian pottery-making methods that were suggested by shards found in an excavation of funeral mounds. Martínez also helped establish a crafts business that revitalized her pueblo in New Mexico.

Ada Deer, chairwoman of the Menominee Restoration Committee, signs a deed returning Menominee land to reservation status on April 23, 1975, as Secretary of the Interior Rogers Morton (left) and others look on.

of the Senate Select Committee on Indian Affairs. La-Donna Harris (Comanche) founded Americans for Indian Opportunity in 1970. The organization advocates natural resource management, improved environmental quality, and efforts toward tribal self-government. Harris served on presidential commissions in the Johnson, Ford, and Carter administrations.

Wilma Mankiller has served as the principal chief of the Cherokee Nation of Oklahoma since 1985. Mankiller, whose family was forced by drought and government incentives to leave their home in Oklahoma for San Francisco, was a social worker and activist in the Native American rights movement in the 1960s. She returned to Oklahoma in 1975 and became director of community development for the Cherokee Nation in 1979. Mankiller initiated programs to develop rural water systems and to rehabilitate houses among poor rural Cherokee. She was elected vice-chief in 1983, rose to the office of chief when her running mate, Ross Swimmer, stepped down to become director of the BIA, and was elected chief in 1987. As the principal chief, Mankiller created a department of commerce that oversees all of the tribe's business enterprises as well as projects to encourage innovative use of tribal lands. She was inducted into Oklahoma's Women's Hall of Fame in 1986, and in 1988 *Ms* magazine named Mankiller one of its Women of the Year.

Cultural Revivalism

More and more, Indians are devoting themselves to recapturing and preserving their heritage. Many young Indians are greatly interested in seeking to understand the spiritual values of their ancestors. Not only is this true on reservations but also in urban communities where Indians have settled in increasing numbers. Many Indians live and work in urban centers but commute regularly to reservations on weekends and other holidays. Religious beliefs are fundamental to Indians in their pursuit of traditional ways. Many Indians have been converted to Christianity but also maintain beliefs and practices of traditional religions. Congress passed the American Indian Religious Freedom Act (1978) to affirm that the First Amendment to the Constitution protects the right of Native Americans to practice their traditional religions.

The focus on cultural revival greatly involves language and its teaching to the young. The loss of language among Indian groups has been going on for many years, but the losses vary enormously from tribe to tribe. Many Indians in remote areas speak their native language to the exclusion of English or Spanish, from which they may have borrowed some words. Others maintain a fluency in both their native tongue and English or Spanish.

Singing, dancing, and drumming have long been important features of Indian ceremonial and social gatherings. Revitalized Indian get-togethers (pow-wows) began again on the Plains in the 1950s and 1960s and have spread across the nation. Now intertribal powwows are held regularly, providing Indians with the opportunity to perform traditional dances and

Young people wearing elaborate costumes participate in a wacipi (dance) at the University of South Dakota. Indians have undertaken a dynamic cultural revitalization that promises to enrich the lives of all North Americans.

songs and to exchange and preserve cultural information. In a very real sense these gatherings are a part of the revival of traditional customs and of cultural revitalization.

The Indians of today are fiercely proud of their traditional ways of life and are pursuing a great initiative to preserve their heritage. Widespread cultural pride has replaced the tendency in the past for Indians to ignore or even hide their ancestry. Indians have undertaken a dynamic cultural revitalization that encompasses the arts, the collection of oral histories, language study, and the development of a number of native studies programs in institutions of higher learning.

In June 1990, an event of enormous importance for Native Americans took place. The Museum of the American Indian–Heye Foundation became a part of the Smithsonian Institution. The new museum, called the National Museum of the American Indian, will open its doors on the Mall in Washington, D.C., in 1998.

Prior to that date, the George Gustav Heye Center will open in the U.S. Custom House in New York City. George Gustav Heye, the museum's founder, obtained his first Native American artifact—a Navajo rawhide shirt—in 1897. The museum's priceless collection represents and symbolizes the greatness and creative genius of Native Americans from the Artic to Tierra del Fuego. Many private citizens and politicians helped make the national museum a reality, including Representative Ben Nighthorse Campbell of Colorado (Northern Cheyenne). The first director of the National Museum of the American Indian is Richard West, Jr., a lawyer and member of the Cheyenne-Arapaho tribes. Both Campbell and West symbolize current Indian leaders across the land.

The Future of American Indians

Indians are proud bearers of their culture today. Some examples of Indian heritage are found in museums, but many are also found in the everyday life of Native Americans. Most Indians are split between two cultures—one native and traditional, the other Western. Some Indian men wear their hair long and favor ribbon shirts and bolo ties. They may also belong to a bowling league and periodically gather with other former servicemen at the local American Legion post. An enormous acculturation has occurred, but medicine bundles (collections of sacred objects believed to be the source of tribal or individual power) are still kept by Plains families. An Inuit drummer at a community dance beats on a traditional circular drum and chants an ancient litany; he is accompanied by dancers wearing blue jeans and sneakers. Contemporary Indian life is a blend, and it is exceptional in its diversity. But this was true before Columbus's arrival. With all the change that has occurred and with all the adversity Indians have faced, some things have changed very little or not at all. Cultural change is always balanced with cultural persistence, and persistence is achieved by individuals.

Appendix: Primary Locations of American Indian Groups

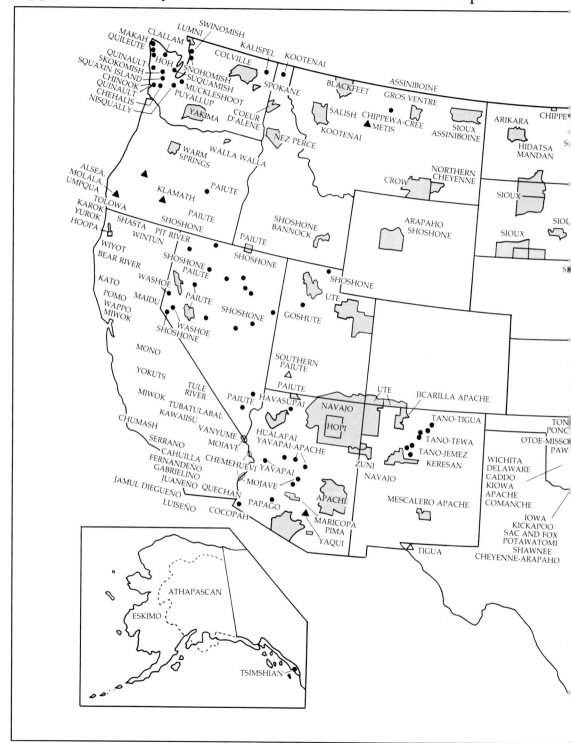

CHIPPEWA

EWA

CHIPPEWA

CHIPPEWA
OTTAWA

CHIPPEWA
OTTAWA

MALECITE   MICMAC
PASSAMAQUODDY
PENOBSCOT

MOHAWK

CHIPPEWA

CHIPPEWA

MENOMINEE
STOCKBRIDGE
MUNSEE

POTAWATOMI

ONEIDA

WINNEBAGO

BROTHERTON

CHIPPEWA

POTAWATOMI

TONAWANDA
TUSCARORA

ONEIDA
ONONDAGA

NIPMUC

CAYUGA

SENECA

PEQUOT

WAMPANOAG
NARRAGANSET
MOHEGAN

PAUGUSETT

SCHAGHTICOKE

MONTAUK
SHINNECOCK
POOSPATUCK

SAC AND FOX

NEBAGO

MIAMI

MOOR

NANTICOKE

SAC AND FOX

KICKAPOO
WYANDOT

ATOMI

PPEWA AND
SEE DELAWARE

OKEE

SAGE

SHAWNEE
MIAMI
PEORIA

QUAPAW
SENECA-CAYUGA
WYANDOT

REEK
INOLE
CTAW
KASAW

RAPPAHANOCK
MATTAPONI

AMHERST
CHICKAHOMINY

PAMUNKEY

CUBAN

HALIWA

COHARIE

CHEROKEE

LUMBEE

WACCAMAW

CATAWBA

SUMMERVILLE

CHOCTAW

CHOCTAW

CHOCTAW

CREEK

ABAMA

TUNICA

COUSHATTA

CHITIMACHA

HOUMA

SEMINOLE

SEMINOLE

MICCOSUKEE

MICCOSUKEE

		Federal Indian Reservations
△		State Indian Reservations
▲		Other Indian Groups

FURTHER READING

Deloria, Vine, Jr., ed. *American Indian Policy in the Twentieth Century.* Norman: University of Oklahoma Press, 1985.

Deloria, Vine, Jr., and Clifford Lytle. *The Nations Within: The Past and Future of American Indian Sovereignty.* New York: Pantheon Books, 1984.

Driver, Harold. *Indians of North America.* Chicago: University of Chicago Press, 1961.

Fagan, Brian M. *The Great Journey: The Peopling of Ancient America.* London: Thames and Hudson, 1987.

Fixico, Donald L. *Termination and Relocation: Federal Indian Policy, 1945–1960.* Albuquerque: University of New Mexico Press, 1986.

Goodman, Jeffrey. *American Genesis: The American Indian and the Origins of Modern Man.* New York: Summit Books, 1981.

Harlan, Judith. *American Indians Today: Issues and Conflicts.* New York: Watts, 1987.

Hirschfelder, Arlene. *Happily May I Walk: American Indians and Alaska Natives Today.* New York: Scribners, 1986.

Hodge, William. *The First Americans: Then and Now.* New York: Holt, Rinehart & Winston, 1981.

Philip, Kenneth R. *John Collier's Crusade for Indian Reform, 1920–1954.* Tucson: The University of Arizona Press, 1977.

Porter, Frank W., III. *The Bureau of Indian Affairs.* New York: Chelsea House, 1988.

Rosenstiel, Annette. *Red and White: Indian Views of the White Man, 1492–1982.* New York: Universe Books, 1983.

Trenton, Patricia, and Patrick T. Houlihan. *Native Americans: Five Centuries of Changing Images.* New York: Abrams, 1989.

U.S. Department of Commerce, Bureau of the Census. *We, the First Americans.* Washington, DC: Government Printing Office, 1989.

Warner, John Anson. *The Life and Art of the North American Indian.* New York: Crescent Books, 1975.

INDEX

PICTURE CREDITS

ROLAND W. FORCE earned his doctorate in anthropology from Stanford University. He served as director of the Bishop Museum in Honolulu from 1962 to 1976. He was director of the Museum of the American Indian in New York from 1977 to June 1990.

MARYANNE TEFFT FORCE has a B.A. and an M.A. in sociology from Stanford University. She completed additional graduate work at Northwestern University and received her Ph.D. in education from Walden University.

The Forces have written numerous anthropological publications together.

DANIEL PATRICK MOYNIHAN is the senior United States senator from New York. He is also the only person in American history to serve in the cabinets or subcabinets of four successive presidents—Kennedy, Johnson, Nixon, and Ford. Formerly a professor of government at Harvard University, he has written and edited many books, including *Beyond the Melting Pot, Ethnicity: Theory and Experience* (both with Nathan Glazer), *Loyalties*, and *Family and Nation*.